NO TIME FOR TEARS

NO TIME FOR TEARS

BY

KATHERYN PATTERSON

JOHNSON PUBLISHING COMPANY

CHICAGO • 1965

Library of Congress Catalog Number 65-23539

In memory of Rosie and Henry Thompson
("Mom" and "Pops")
and dedicated to my mother,
Doreather Killion Givens

CONTENTS

Appendix

Prologue

BLACK DAY

IT WAS a warm spring morning, the kind of day that my three-year-old daughter, Karen, called a "happy time day". But it was not a "happy time day" for me. This was the day I was to learn *why* my eight-week-old son's head had grown several inches since his birth. This was the day that I had dreaded since the pediatrician had called in the neurologist for consultation when I brought "Junior" in for his six weeks check-up. This was the day that followed a sleepless night of talking, second-guessing and wishful thinking with my husband, Pat. However hard we tried to cheer each other up and hope for the best, the memory of our tiny son, his head shaven and punctured by many needles, filled us with fear and foreboding.

We got up early. Pat wanted to take the day off from work to go to the hospital with me. I wanted him to be there with me, too. But, much as I needed him, I felt I should not give in to the feeling. Our debts were mounting, and Junior's hospitalization coming so soon after my confinement meant that we could not afford to lose a day's pay. When he got ready to leave for work, he held me close, and kissed me. I started to tremble, and then, I suppose because he thought he would break down too, he left the house.

I was in such a hurry to get to the hospital that I called a taxi. My grandmother, "Mom," knew I was worried, but she kept busy, and said nothing. I waited impatiently for the taxi, silently thanking my grandmother, who had been a tower of strength for me all of my life, for just being there. Driving to the hospital I looked out at the green Midway, the broad parkway that connects Washington and Jackson Parks. The University of Chicago buildings gave a reassuring impression of strength and solidity. Surely nothing could go wrong here.

I entered the lobby of Bobs Roberts Children's Hospital and walked slowly to the elevator. I had been rushing before, but now I moved slowly. As I left the elevator, I was met by the sounds of children laughing and playing, and babies crying. I imagined I could hear my baby crying for me. This was foolish, since he was too young even to know who I was. The pediatrics ward was bright and cheerful, a small world for the many youngsters for whom it was a temporary home. I could see my baby before I reached the doorway. He was so still and pale that I found myself wishing that he had been one of the crying babies. I stood helplessly by his crib. I could not and did not want to think beyond that moment. I looked at my child and knew how much I was afraid.

Then the doctor was behind me. "Will you please step across the hall?" The tone of his voice gave me no cause to hope. He opened the door to what must have been a conference room. I took a seat in a straight-backed chair. There was a portable blackboard which he used for diagrams. The doctor had an air of professional efficiency which inspired confidence that he knew his business, but he did not radiate warmth and understanding. He pointed to the diagram and proceeded to explain my child's condition. The illustration was of a large head, and there was something in it that looked like a tube. The passageway for the spinal fluid was blocked, he explained. This prevented the fluid flowing from the brain to the spinal cord, and caused an abnormal enlargement of the head.

I heard the doctor's words but he could have been speaking to a stranger. From far away I heard him say that the baby might not live because of the rate of growth of the head. I walked out of the room before he finished his explanation. I don't remember leaving the hospital. I don't remember whether I took a taxi, a bus, or whether I walked home. My grandmother was sitting in a chair sewing when I came in. I fell on my knees, sobbing, and she let me cry until I could talk rationally.

Every time I thought of telling Pat, I started crying again. He had wanted a boy, a namesake, more than anything in the world. I knew I had to tell him as soon as he came home. When he came in I started telling him as much as I could remember. Pat was standing by the refrigerator in the kitchen. When I told him that the doctor said it was doubtful if "Junior" would live, he leaned against the refrigerator, and cried, "My God, no!" That was the first time I had seen my husband cry.

PART I

Life Before Junior

CENTRALIA

WHY DID THIS have to happen to me? After I recovered from the first shock of learning about our baby's abnormality I began, at first bitterly and resentfully, to wonder what I had done to deserve or to cause such a terrible thing to happen. I was 19 years old when Junior was born, and felt I had already had my share of illness and unhappiness. As I struggled to adjust to the new situation I thought a lot about my own childhood.

I was born in Centralia, a small town in southern Illinois, on June 5th, 1936. I was an only child and my mother and father, Doreather and Ivan Killion, lived with my maternal grandparents. As long as they lived my grandfather and grandmother ("Pops" and "Mom") were a never failing source of affection and help. Their very different personalities live in all my childhood memories.

Pops was always good to me, never too busy to have time to give me. As I grew up I heard people criticize him; they said that he never saved a dime, though he was a hard worker and earned good money at the Illinois Central Round House in Centralia. But Pops believed in enjoying his worldly possessions while he was still alive. His voice was husky and his laugh hearty and he didn't take life too seriously. All the same, he was in church every Sunday—all day if there was some special program—and at prayer meetings on Wednesday nights. Although he wasn't an educated man, he knew his Bible and was a devout member of the New Bethel Baptist Church in Centralia, and of the Baptist faith. He was a deacon in the church, and chairman of the Deacon's Board for years. I used to love going along with Mom and Pops to night service on Sundays, and I can remember being carried home in Pops' arms every Sunday night, drowsy and only half aware of his steady reassuring footsteps along the road home.

Mom was almost completely opposite to Pops. He was always a snappy dresser—she dressed very plainly and simply, and never wore makeup of any kind. In church or at home Pops was always long-winded in his prayers, and loud and fervent with his Amens. Mom was deeply religious, but to her it was not a public matter. She used to say that her talks with God were very private: "I can never be lonely, because I have a friend I can call on without appointment, day or night. My God is always willing to talk things over with me." And you could tell how she felt by just looking at the expression on her face when she talked about God.

Mom was goodnatured, but she was very plain and outspoken. She hated to be idle and she used to tell me, "An idle mind is the devil's workshop." I don't know where she heard that, but her life certainly reflected her belief in it. Her unwavering sense of duty toward God and her steadiness and faith never failed her. In the years ahead it was Mom to whom I so often turned for comfort and guidance. From infancy, I loved both my grandparents with all my heart.

The first four years of my life were spent in the 800 block on East Haussler Street. It was dusty and unpaved, but because I had never lived anywhere else I didn't give the dust any thought. I was happy to spend my days in our yard, and in our neighbors' yards, just playing. It was during that time, though, that I had the first big scare in my life, an experience which is still horrifyingly clear and sharp in my memory.

Six of us, boys and girls of pre-school age, were sitting on the ground one day, doing nothing. It was hot. I said "Let's play hide and seek." Everyone yelled "OK" and before any one else could speak I hollered "I'll be it."

The day before while playing some game, two of my friends, Talmadge and Leslie, had made me angry. I told them then, "I'll get even with you." The next day they had forgotten the incident, but I had not. Talmadge and Leslie made the mistake of hiding in an old trunk that was on our back porch. I decided to scare them a little. So

I locked them in the trunk. After a short while I decided to let them out. The trunk was stuck. I was so scared I was nearly speechless. My mother was over at my Grandmother Killion's. I ran for her as fast as my four-year-old legs would carry me, screaming every step of the way, "Muh, Muh, Muh!" She knew something was terribly wrong by my shrieks and the terror in my eyes. I took her hand and dragged her all the way home. All I could do was point to the trunk. She still did not know exactly what I was jabbering about, but when she opened the trunk I know she must have been horrified by what she saw. Talmadge and Leslie had both changed color and begun to foam at the mouth. Mother got them out of the trunk and they began to revive. She put cold cloths on their heads and finally when she felt they were going to be all right she told me to get in the house and stay there until she could get to me. It was agony waiting for her and I felt it was punishment enough for me to have seen the two children like that, but Mother didn't think so. She gave me my first whipping. I made a big mistake and ran. She caught me and when she did, she made it impossible for me to sit comfortably for quite some time. She also impressed upon me that I had almost done something that I would have regretted all of my life. Pops became angry with Mother for spanking me so hard. Pops often interceded for me and was the cause of me escaping some of the spankings I deserved.

We were all sitting on the back steps one day when Pops came in with some big news. "Kids," he said, "we are moving." My first reaction was, "No, we can't do that." I looked up at Pops and asked, "Are my friends going to move with us?" He said, "No baby, but we will come over here to see them often." I wasn't very happy about this bit of news. I loved dusty, familiar Haussler Street where we had so much fun, but it did not take me long to get used to the idea of moving. Moving day was one big party for me.

The new house Pops had bought was across town on North Locust Street. I was so excited. To my eyes, Locust Street was the most beautiful street in the world. Big trees lined both sides of the street. The yards were all so pretty and green. Even the alleys were clean and free from dust.

Uncle Wilbert, Mother's young brother, and I explored the new neighborhood from top to bottom, end to end. We were awed by it all. We could see the Illinois Central Railroad tracks from our front yard. We lived only a block from the tracks and we loved watching the trains go by. We learned to tell the time of day by which train was going by. Other times we would sit out under the big tree in our front yard and count the cars going north or south on Highway 51, which ran right in front of our house. This was especially fun after heavy rain. The street always flooded after a rain and the cars would zoom through the water, splashing it on the curb. We would squeal with delight. To some, this may not sound very exciting, but to two kids who had never seen anything like it, it was great. Everything always smelled so good after a rain. Good, clean, fresh air, and everything looking greener and prettier than before.

Soon we made our first friend from Locust Street, Maurice Green. Immediately we were a team of three. I was the youngest, but I tagged along with them anyway. Being boys, they made me do all the things they did not like to do. I was eager to please, so I obeyed. I was "initiated" at least once a week. I had to do as they told me if I wanted to be one of the fellows. My first lesson provided me with quite an education. The boys made me smoke a green cigar from the tree in the side yard. This experience was enough for me; to this day I am a dedicated non-smoker.

One day in March, 1947, when I was ten years old, I was with a couple of girls on the front walk when the worst disaster in Centralia's history occurred. Mining at that time was nearly as big an industry in the town as the Illinois Central Railroad. On that Tuesday the No. 5 mine exploded. There was a hush over Centralia that even the smallest child could feel. I heard people on the street talking about all the lives that had been lost, and about the many bereaved families. I could feel the rising excitement and tension as the whole town became aware of the tragedy, even though I suppose I couldn't have understood the magnitude of the horror at the time. Looking back on it now I know how terrible the grief of these families must have been, and I can remember the warmth and friendliness of Centralia's citizens in this time of crisis. This memory helps me toward a sense of proportion about my own experiences there as an adolescent girl, and later as a young mother.

PARENTS AND SCHOOLDAYS

IN THE SPRING of 1941 when I was five years old, my mother left home. She took me in her arms and for a few seconds she almost squeezed the breath out of me. Mother and I had always been close. She had never failed to let me know how delighted she was to have me for her daughter. On the other hand, from a very young child, I was aware that Dad would have preferred his only child to be a son. This day I was puzzled. I said, "Muh, Muh, what's the matter?" The strain in her voice made it difficult for me to understand her. She was trembling as she said, "Baby, Muh is going on a long vacation. But, while I'm gone, how would you like to receive special packages and mail, even though it won't be your birthday or anything?" The excitement of looking forward to unexpected gifts dulled the shock of mother's leaving, and she tried as best she could to soften the blow.

Mother only stayed away for a few months, and during this time I believe Dad did his best to fill the emptiness in my life. He bought me new clothes, for I was to start school at the end of that summer, but though he was generous he was never able to communicate any affection to me. If he had just once taken me on his knee and said, "Daddy loves you, Baby," my life would have been quite different.

Looking back now I can see that it was difficult for him, too. Dad was a good-looking man. He was very fair-complexioned, and had been encouraged by his mother and other women to think too much of his good looks and his charm. He was very popular outside his family, and consequently too busy to give us the attention we needed. Also, and probably more important for him than any other consideration, he had badly wanted a son, and until shortly before his death was never able to take pleasure in having a daughter.

On the first day of school I was very much aware of the other mothers taking their children to school. Mom came with me, but I felt Mother's absence very strongly, and envied the other children. By this time the excitement of the letters and packages had worn off. Every night when the lights were out I cried into my pillow, and every morning when I woke up there was a feeling of something being wrong, followed by a sensation of emptiness as I realized what it was. My father was beginning to show impatience with my whining.

When mother did come home again, I was overjoyed.

Years later, I learned that Mother and Dad had decided

to stay together, for my sake, until I was grown and married. I don't know what their differences were, but I shall always be grateful for the decision that they made.

Although I was much happier with Mother home again, my parents' separation had changed me from a happy and healthy little girl into an insecure and sickly child. Dad was away from home much of the time because of his job as a porter on the Illinois Central Railroad, but I was used to his absence and now that Mother was back in Centralia, all should have been well. I know that my parents contrived somehow to shield me from any knowledge of their disagreements. It was not until I was twelve years old that I heard them quarrel, and this was both the first and last time. It was on Christmas Eve and I heard their voices in the kitchen from my room upstairs. I came downstairs and though I didn't know what the argument was about, I couldn't believe my eyes as I stood in the doorway watching them. It frightened me so much that I ran, barefoot, to Mom's house, and she telephoned them later to come and fetch me home.

In this period of ill-health, in addition to my full share of the usual childhood diseases, I became subject to attacks of bronchial asthma, and also became alarmingly accident prone. The most serious of these mishaps occurred in the playground of the Lincoln School. The swings there were good and sturdy, and one day, sharing a swing with my friend Dorothy, my enthusiasm pushed us right over the top bar and out into the playground. Both of us were covered with cuts and bruises, and I knocked a hole in my chin. This incident subdued me for a while, and I managed to stay out of trouble for the rest of the summer, but when school started again in the fall I got into a different kind of trouble. Each class was to have a girl and boy representative to compete as king and queen of the school carnival. Against my mother's wishes I accepted the nomination from my class. It was a fund-raising event and I felt sure I could raise a fortune. Well, you have never seen a mother as humiliated as mine the night of the crowning. The total sum that I had raised was sixty-seven cents, from returning pop bottles for the deposit. When my name was called, my mother was astounded and ashamed. Of course, my backside caught it once again. Now that I am a mother, I must admit it was well deserved.

I stayed in hot water and kept my mother in a dither over my determination to keep up with the gang. My distaste for dresses increased with each day. After all, you can't do tricks on a bike with a dress on, or climb trees either. I was still under the sponsorship of Maurice Green and my Uncle Wilbert. Maurice taught me bike tricks and Uncle Wilbert taught me how to fight. I didn't like to fight much, so I learned to talk fast. That was a lot easier.

Then my cousin Adrienne came to live with us for a while. This was a good thing for me. I had to learn to share the affection of Mother, Mom and Pops with her. Adrienne, my mother's sister's daughter, was two years younger than I, so we started doing everything together. Our first big escapade was when we played barber shop and cut off each other's hair. We looked horrible, and of course the whole thing was my idea. Adrienne and I would fight each other, but developed a sense of loyalty that prevented us from allowing anyone else to fight one without the other getting in the act. By the end of Adrienne's visit with us, she was as much of a tomboy as I.

By the time I was in sixth grade the home economics class had become more appealing to me than playing basketball with the boys. I could feel the change coming over me, but I didn't know what it was. Suddenly, however, I was taking an interest in "the young lady side of me."

My mother wisely allowed me to make the transition from childhood to adolescence in the easiest and most natural way. The summer before I entered eighth grade was very full and exciting. I was still a tomboy, and had more than my share of accidents, but the entrancing world of bike rides, days at the beach, and going everywhere with the gang was opening up for me, and I was busy and active all through the long summer days.

There were bruises in that period, both physical and emotional. I twice suffered quite severe head injuries, the first time when I was thrown from my bike when I hit a bump in the road, and again when I was accidentally hit by a baseball bat. A deeper hurt occurred at my graduation. As I entered the eighth grade I was beginning to hope that Dad and I were getting closer. One spring evening we were sitting on the porch, and Dad started to talk about my approaching graduation. He told me he was proud of my good grades, and promised me a wonderful graduation present. When the day came and my name was called I looked over to where my parents were to be; they were supposed to stand as I received my diploma and I didn't know till that moment that Dad had not bothered to come. Mother was there, with Pops standing with her. Dad never explained why he hadn't come, and from that time I gave up looking to my father for affection and support. Increasingly I turned to Pops, who was always there when I needed him, and, having no education himself, always encouraged me to get the most I could out of school.

ADOLESCENCE AND ILLNESS

IN THE SPRING of 1948, when I was thirteen, Mother allowed me to go out with Dorothy, one of my best friends, and her brother Cecil, who was two years older than we were. People criticized my mother for allowing me to date so young, but she felt that I could go places with Cecil that she could not take me, and that he was a nice boy, who could be trusted to take care of me. Mother was right; Cecil was always a gentleman and a very good friend. At my graduation from elementary school, he had comforted me for my father's absence.

During that summer, although it was a happy one, I first began to have severe headaches, and was sick off and on all through the time until I entered high school in September. I had been looking forward to high school, and it lived up to my expectations. I couldn't have been happier.

My freshman year just sailed by. My grades were good and, since English was one of my better subjects, my English teacher suggested I try out for the staff of the school paper, *The Sphinx Weekly*. I enjoyed work on the newspaper and on the yearbook, *The Sphinx Annual,* and various other extra-curricular activities, including going to ball games for the first time without an adult. Centralia was a very sportsminded town, with enthusiastic followings for both the basketball and baseball teams.

Summer passed quickly, and as I returned to school for my sophomore year, I was burning with ambition. I wanted to do so much. I wanted to hurry and be old enough to start a career. I decided to take extra subjects and try to finish high school in three years.

I was on the committee in charge of decorations for the homecoming dance, and though I wasn't much of a football fan, I did enjoy the dances that followed the games. Excitement always ran high before the games, both football and basketball. At one semi-final in Centralia's holiday basbetball tournament, the competition was rough and the game went into a double overtime. I screamed and screamed until I was hoarse, but the excitement proved to be too much for me. Just as Centralia won the game, I fainted.

From this point on my health went downhill. In January I had appendicitis. The night before surgery I was petrified with fear. I don't think anyone realized how scared I was.

My fears intensified as the mask was placed over my nose.

Everything was closing in on me. I was floating away. I was calling for help. No one would answer me. Nothing seemed to matter. Suddenly, there was no pain. Nothing. Then, voices far away were drifting closer and closer to me. I began to feel I was falling. I couldn't stop tumbling over and over again. I hit bottom and opened my eyes. I was deathly afraid. Mother was standing over me smiling. She said one word, "Hi." That was the most beautiful sound in the world. I knew that the nightmare was over. I fell into a deep restful sleep.

Once I was home again complications set in. At first I could not walk at all. When I did begin walking, my left leg was stiff and swollen to twice its normal size. My doctor was baffled. He was a physician and surgeon, and he did not see my problem as emotional rather than physical. He could not find anything organically wrong with me, and I returned to school. Because I limped as I walked, I was a target for cruel jokes and insults. Once for a joke, I was tripped and fell down a flight of stairs. The laughter was hilarious. Young people don't realize how cruel they are being, or that the hurts they inflict go deeper than the injury or humiliation of the moment.

Due to my operation and the long convalescent period I fell behind in most of my classwork. I was carrying an extra class load because I wanted to graduate from high school in three years. I began to have violent headaches. Soon after I returned to school I started having fainting spells. The Dean of Girls thought my work load was too heavy, and at her suggestion I dropped two subjects. This didn't help me. I continued to faint, sometimes as often as five or six times a day. Most of the time there was no warning that I was going to faint. Mother never knew when she was going to get a call to come and get me. I would faint in class and between classes. This went on for several weeks. The fainting spells were soon accompanied by convulsions.

My parents' friends and some members of dad's family told mother I was crazy. They didn't offer help or comfort, only gratuitous advice. Mother really needed the consolation of friends and she had two who were loyal: her cousin Earlene Coleman who lived across the street, with her husband, Wilson. They were always on hand when she needed them, not only to help with me, but to talk with her. Another good friend who stuck by us was Annis Downey. Thinking back now, it seems as though Annis was always at our house. My Locust Street buddies, Twanette and Peggy Giboney, Margaret Bibbs and Georgia Mae Hutchinson remained loyal to me. Neither Mother nor I realized at the time how much the friendship of these people would mean to us in the future. Most of all though, the unfailing support and love we had from Mom and Pops gave us the only real security we had during the years of my illness.

My father had no patience with me. Every time he spoke to me he criticized or scolded me. One day, as I came in from school, he jumped down my throat about some trivial thing and I turned on him. I attacked him with a broom. He was entertaining a friend and the incident provoked him to say he wanted nothing more to do with me, and would refuse to help Mother in any way.

Mother went out, sat on the back steps, and cried. As she was sitting there, discouraged and absorbed in her misery, Mrs. Walker (wife of the school principal and a social worker in town) walked across the school yard to speak to her. Mrs. Walker began to talk to her about me; she asked if we had any money, and this renewed Mother's distress. She knew I needed professional help, but we couldn't afford it. All she had been able to do was to hope daily that she could see some signs of improvement, or that someone would somehow help. And at this point she needed a shoulder to cry on to relieve her own misery.

Mrs. Walker was sympathetic as well as able to offer constructive help. She said she would get in touch with the rehabilitation center in Mount Vernon, Illinois, and they would contact us. "I know how much Katheryn means to you," she said, "and how concerned you have been."

It was not long before an interviewer, a psychologist, was sent by the rehabilitation center to see me in Centralia. As he talked to me he could see my excitability, and how disturbed I was about the changes that were happening to me, which I could not understand or control. As the interview went on I became more and more upset, and finally went into a seizure.

As a result of this interview it was arranged that I should attend the Illinois Research Hospital in Chicago, as an outpatient. At first this meant daily trips to the hospital, which of course were strenuous and upsetting for both mother and me. Mom's sister, Aunt Helen, lived near the hospital and opened her home and her heart to us. She is very like Mom, quiet in manner, and she was of great comfort to us.

The first time I went into the hospital I was plain scared. These trips to the clinic were for extensive tests. Mother couldn't go with me to the testing room. In this very small cold room I was given a pill, which was to relax me and put me in a deep sleep. This was necessary in order to give me an electroencephalograph—a brain wave test. I could feel myself drifting off to sleep. It was as though all the tension in me was being released. I enjoyed this, though I was always groggy for a short while afterwards. After days and long hours of testing, mother received heartbreaking news. I was an epileptic.

Mother, Mom and Pops tried to make life as pleasant for me as humanly possible. It was a frustrating job. I was becoming more and more withdrawn, and harder to handle each day. Mom suggested a change of scene might help. I was behind in school anyway, and my frame of mind was not good. She took me to Chicago for a month's vacation.

I knew a boy from Chicago, whom I had met during the holiday tournament in Centralia. Though I was sick a lot, and I couldn't date too often, because of the frequency of my seizures, I was otherwise a normal teenager. Tony——— and I had been corresponding and he had come to Centralia to visit me right after my operation. So, on my arrival in Chicago I called him. Tony took me out and introduced me to his family and friends. I fainted several times when I was with Tony and his family, and I'm sure it was very embarrassing for him. He always treated me with consideration, and proved to be a good friend. Between attacks I did enjoy my Chicago vacation, which seemed all too short.

The change in my attitude which had been possible in Chicago, where I had escaped for a time from the stares and comments of familiar people, did not long survive the return to Centralia. I had missed so much class work that my return to school was doubly hard; my work load had been lightened, but my seizures were worse.

My classmates, even those who had been my friends, did nothing to help me. I was whispered about and avoided. I was no longer invited to parties. I felt curiosity and rejection, but no sympathy. I have often wondered why there was such a lack of understanding of my problem, but I could not escape my role as the oddball, the pariah—and of course this made my nervous condition worse.

The headaches I had become used to were now relieved by taking phenobarbital and dilantin, but the seizures continued. One of the worst occurred when I was rehearsing with my class for the Centralia High School's May Fete. Once again, Mother was called, but this was to be the last time. As I lay on a cot I heard the Dean of Girls talking to my mother: "Katheryn is a very alert girl and capable of catching up, I'm sure . . . but the school feels it would be too much of a risk for Katheryn, and for us, if she were to continue in school in her present condition."

LOVE AND MARRIAGE

DESPONDENT, defeated and bitter though I felt, I took my troubles and my disappointment that same afternoon to Miss Claybrook, the wonderful woman who had been my third grade teacher. She had always been an inspiration to me, her interest and patience had never failed, and now, as always, she tried to give me hope.

"Kathy, I know you are hurt now, so cry it out of your system and come out with that old determination. An education is important to you, I know, but knowing you, I am sure that this blow will only slow you down. I am still very proud of you. Remember you are not alone. Have faith. You have the friendship of almighty God when there is no one else."

I heard what she said, but the words meant nothing to me then. I felt I had been treated unfairly, and as I brooded on my fate, with too much time on my hands, my bitterness increased, and with it my seizures.

With nothing to occupy the long days, my life was aimless and unsatisfactory. I was an object of gossip, and painfully conscious of it. I knew that people were saying I was mad, and that Mother was mad herself for putting up with me. The effect of being debarred from school, of being avoided by my former classmates, and of feeling that my place in life was rapidly becoming that of the town freak was to keep me in a state of near hysteria. When I did go to the place where the teenagers danced, I was easily goaded into fights. The kids knew that if they got me excited I would fight anyone —boy or girl, man or woman. At this time only my friends from Locust Street stuck with me. Maurice became my protector, and watched over me like a big brother.

My emotional state was becoming so bad that Mother decided to take me back to Chicago for another examination, and also to give me a break from Centralia. The trip did more than that for me; at a time when everything seemed hopeless, I met the person who was to give my life a real meaning and purpose.

One weekend during that June of 1952, my friend Twanette, who was also in Chicago visiting relatives, invited me over. Knowing that Twanette was familiar with my seizures, Mother allowed me to go. I was excited when I arrived and Twanette told me she had a blind date for me.

My first reaction to Delbert Patterson was one of acute embarrassment. He seemed so cool and self-assured. I didn't know how to match his calm assurance, and my first instinct was to run away. However, after the first shock of introduction was over we went out to dinner with Twanette and Delbert's brother. All evening I felt inadequate and tense. The date had not come up to my expectations, so I was surprised when Delbert called the next evening and suggested going to the movies. First telling him that I was epileptic and warning him that I could be taken ill, Mother allowed me to go. During that evening I learned that Delbert was much less cocky than he had seemed—he covered a soft heart and a sympathetic personality with apparent self-confidence. I also learned to call him Pat rather than Delbert. We came home early from the show and Pat stayed and talked for some time.

Pat was born in DuQuoin, a small town in southern Illinois about forty miles from Centralia, which he had often visited as a teenager. The Pattersons lived on a large farm in DuQuoin, and they were a large family. With three sisters, Helen, Wilma, and Lowanda, and two brothers, Andrew and Henry, Pat had been raised by his dad, Henry Patterson, Sr., since his mother had died when he was only three weeks old. Pat was closest in age and affection to his brother Henry, and he could talk for hours about their adventures together. I could tell that Pat had always longed for his mother, whom he must resemble in his sympathetic and affectionate disposition, for his father was a hard man, who showed little love to his children. Of course this reminded me of my own father, and increased our mutual sympathy.

As the children grew up they left home, one by one, and I could sympathize with their desire to escape. But Henry Patterson, though unaffectionate to his children, was a hard-working man, and he taught his children to value honest work, to live up to their responsibilities, and to be loyal to one another. People I have talked to about Pat's mother, Isabelle Merrell Patterson, have told me that she was a much warmer person, easygoing, understanding, and compassionate. This is easy for me to believe for I have seen her sweet nature in her last son.

As Pat and I continued to see each other I saw always fresh evidence of the disposition he had inherited from his mother. He always carried my medicine and smelling salts with him. The whispers and stares that we encountered didn't worry him, and he never once deserted me. When I was taken ill, he would pick me up as if I were fragile china. How could I help but fall in love with him?

One hot afternoon about a month later I was sitting on the steps in front of my Aunt Helen's house. It was a couple of hours before I could expect Pat, so when some young people I had met in the neighborhood came by and asked me to go swimming, I grabbed my swimming suit at once. I knew I should not have gone to swim immediately after eating lunch, but I didn't think, and it almost cost me my life. As I was swimming across the eight-foot pool at Stamford Park, I felt a violent cramp in my stomach. Before the lifeguards could reach me I had swallowed quite a bit of water and I was rushed to Cook County Hospital, unconscious.

I was kept in the hospital overnight for observation, and at first I felt too ill to care where I was. Toward morning, however, I heard screaming, and disjointed talking. I sat up, and was unnerved by the discovery that my bed had bars. Next I looked across the aisle to where an old lady was lying in what seemed to be a blood-filled bed. This sight, and the sounds in the ward, which I realized was the psychopathic ward, terrified me. I had been accommodated there because of shortage of space, but all I could think of was getting out of the horrifying situation. I pulled down the guard rails, and with only the brief hospital gown on, ran down the hall to call Mother. All I could say was "Mother, please come and get me." As soon as she could get transportation to the hospital, she did.

Pat and I continued to date. He was twenty-two, with a two-year Navy hitch behind him, young, energetic, good-looking and with a normal ex-sailor's share of experience. I was sixteen, inexperienced and mistrustful of the world, sensitive about my illness and very vulnerable to both affection and rejection. Many young men would have taken advantage of a young girl with my particular problems, but Pat, against the advice of both family and friends, continued to treat me with patience and understanding. We both knew what the experts said about teenage marriages and fought against falling in love.

As the protests and objections of friends, both mine and Pat's, were growing, our feeling for each other grew stronger. In spite of the fact that on almost every date I would have a seizure, and sometimes behaved very strangely, Pat made me feel that I was something very special to him, and that I belonged to the human race again. It was a miracle for both of us and nobody could talk us out of our marriage, which we both truly believed was made in heaven.

We were married from the house of Pat's sister, Helen. It was a very simple wedding, with only two of Pat's relatives, my brother-in-law, Andrew, and Mother. I believe that only Pat and I were happy; like most young couples we began our marriage very much in love (and very much in debt), determined to prove that the experts, our family, and our friends, were wrong.

The early days of our marriage provided more ammunition for the doubters than for our supporters. Soon after our marriage we made a trip to Centralia, where Mother and Mom had decided to give a shower for me. We hadn't been able to afford a honeymoon, so I was quite excited about the trip, as well as grateful for the trouble that my mother and grandmother were taking. The general feeling in town, however, was not difficult to interpret. There was no friendliness in the attitude of the people I met, and when I walked into the recreation room of the church where the shower was to be held, there were only four people present, and two of these were Mother and Mom. As the five of us were sitting there trying to make conversation, I looked up and saw Twanette and Peggy standing in the door. I could have kissed them. We talked for a few minutes, and though they were embarrassed for me they sincerely wanted to stay. I persuaded them to leave, because

I didn't want my friends to have to share my humiliation. It was bad enough trying to keep a smile fixed on my face for the sake of Mother and Mom; I was particularly upset for Mom, who was such a dedicated church worker, never refusing her services.

After our return to Chicago, the memory of this incident and other evidences of hostility combined with my own inactivity and the epileptic seizures I was still suffering to put me into a state of depression. Pat's family was still unfriendly; I was pregnant, and resentful of my pregnancy; Pat was away all day, and quiet and withdrawn when he was home in the evenings. I had all day to devote to thinking about my troubles, and I began to wonder if our marriage had been a mistake, and to wish vainly for acceptance both in Centralia and from Pat's family.

My state of mind was at its worst. Every day I became more disheartened and the slightest physical or emotional distress would bring on a seizure. I often fell, and knowing that Pat was unhappy too I felt trapped and frustrated. One night when we were staying with Pat's brother Andrew, Pat was unusually curt with me and my depression got the better of me. I got up, went to the bathroom, and locked the door. I took what I thought were barbiturate pills from the medicine cabinet, swallowed all that were there, and within minutes I passed out. Pat heard me fall; finding the door locked, he got a ladder and climbed in through the window. In hospital, where my stomach was pumped, I was full of remorse. As I lay on the table in the emergency room I was praying to God to forgive me.

My suicide attempt shocked Pat, as well as myself, into a new frame of mind. Mother came to Chicago to stay with us for a while, and during the six months that she was with us, going home only at weekends, she and Pat formed a very close bond. Unlike most in-laws, Mother was a great help in preserving our marriage. She took over the housework, gave us financial help, and by her presence relieved some of the tension and difficulty between us.

When I was six months pregnant I fell down a flight of stairs, and was afraid I would lose the baby. God was with us, and I carried our baby full term.

KAREN

ON MARCH 24th, 1953, my daughter Karen was born. She was a fine big baby of 8 pounds 13½ ounces, and we were very proud of her. As I lay in the recovery room of the Chicago Lying-In Hospital, Miss Claybrook's words came back to me. My life had indeed taken a different turn from what I had planned. At seventeen I was a wife and mother, the first and most difficult period of my marriage was behind me. From the time of Karen's birth, my epileptic seizures vanished.

Pat and I were so happy to have survived the stresses and strains, the hostility of the world and my own ill-health, and to be rediscovering our love for each other. One month after Karen was born, Mother went home. We moved into a new apartment and started real housekeeping for the first time. I enjoyed learning all about Karen, and how to take care of her. I made some mistakes, but we were both growing and learning together.

When Karen was three months old, we took her home to Centralia for a weekend visit. For the first time in many years I felt some friendliness in the people I met; some even welcomed us home. We were really sorry to leave on Sunday afternoon. Our car was old, and the tires were in bad shape. We had three blow-outs between Centralia and Ramsey, Illinois, the last one almost sending the car over a steep embankment. Shakily and carefully we got out of the car and, carrying the baby, I walked a short distance to the nearest farm house and telephoned mother. Mother and Dad asked a friend to drive them the 35 miles to where we were stranded, and they took Karen back to Centralia while Pat and I made our way on to Chicago.

Mother kept Karen for the next two years so that I could get a job, and so that Pat and I could have a second chance to get acquainted and to build a life together. The first three years of Karen's life were as normal as could be. I did quite well in my jobs. I started in a mail-order house and finally got a job as a long-distance telephone operator for A. T. & T., which meant that I could call Mother and Karen every day. Most weekends they travelled up to Chicago to see us, and it seemed that she grew perceptibly with every visit.

One weekend when I didn't have to work I decided to go home before Mother could set off to visit us. I had an uneasy feeling, which I couldn't explain, as I made the trip home, and when I walked into the living-room I saw that it was justified.

Boxes were all over the place, and Mother was packing up everything to bring herself and Karen to live with us in Chicago. I was shocked. I had thought that in the past few years Mother and Dad had become closer, and although Dad had never shown me much love, when he first saw Karen, at six weeks old, he fell in love with her. By the time she was two years old she had him wrapped around her little finger. She was crazy about "gramps" and he gave her all the love he hadn't been able to give to me.

I was wrong. They told me that they were separating for good, that this was to be the end of their marriage, and that they had only stayed together until they were sure that my own marriage was happy. So, in silence and not believing that Dad really wanted the separation, I pitched in and helped with the packing.

It was a joy having Karen home again. A healthy two-year-old is a delight. She loved to entertain us, and Pat and I were a willing and attentive audience. Our little family was happy.

In March of 1955, on Karen's second birthday, Pat had major surgery at the Chicago Veteran's Hospital. Karen was company for me in the long nights when I was waiting for him to come home again; we became very close and I don't know what I would have done without her. In May it was Karen's turn to be hospitalized, with bronchitis. The spring seemed long with Pat recuperating from surgery and Karen ill, but the summer was full of hope. The family was back to its normal health, and I became pregnant. We looked forward with great anticipation to the birth of our second child. We were sure it would be boy, a second Delbert, and immediately started to call him Junior.

PART II

The Patterson Family in Pictures

unior reads,

plays records,

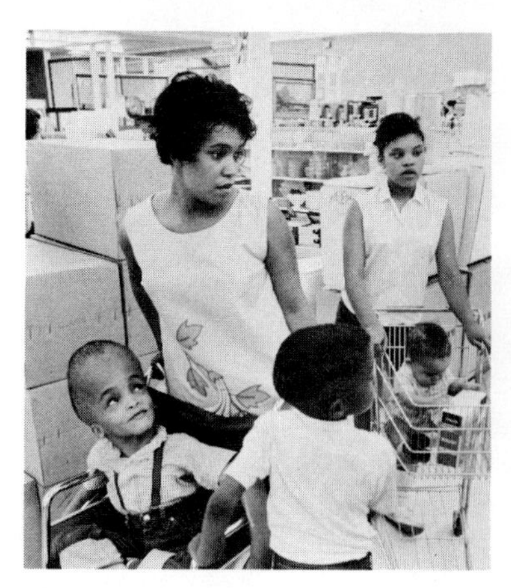

and shops, with his mother

Junior on the swings,

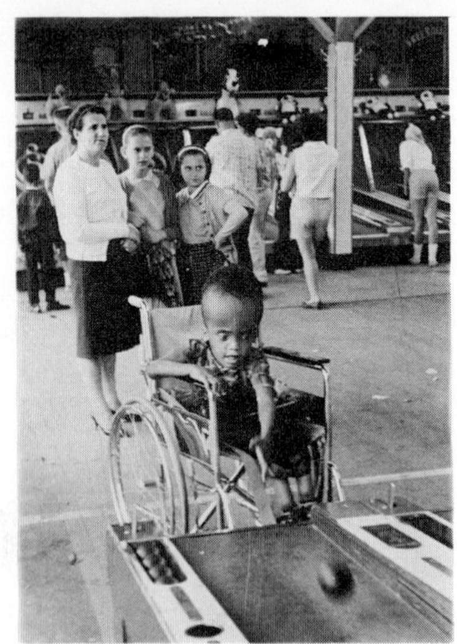

at Riverview Amusement Park,

and playing baseball with his fath
Delbert Patterson, Sr.

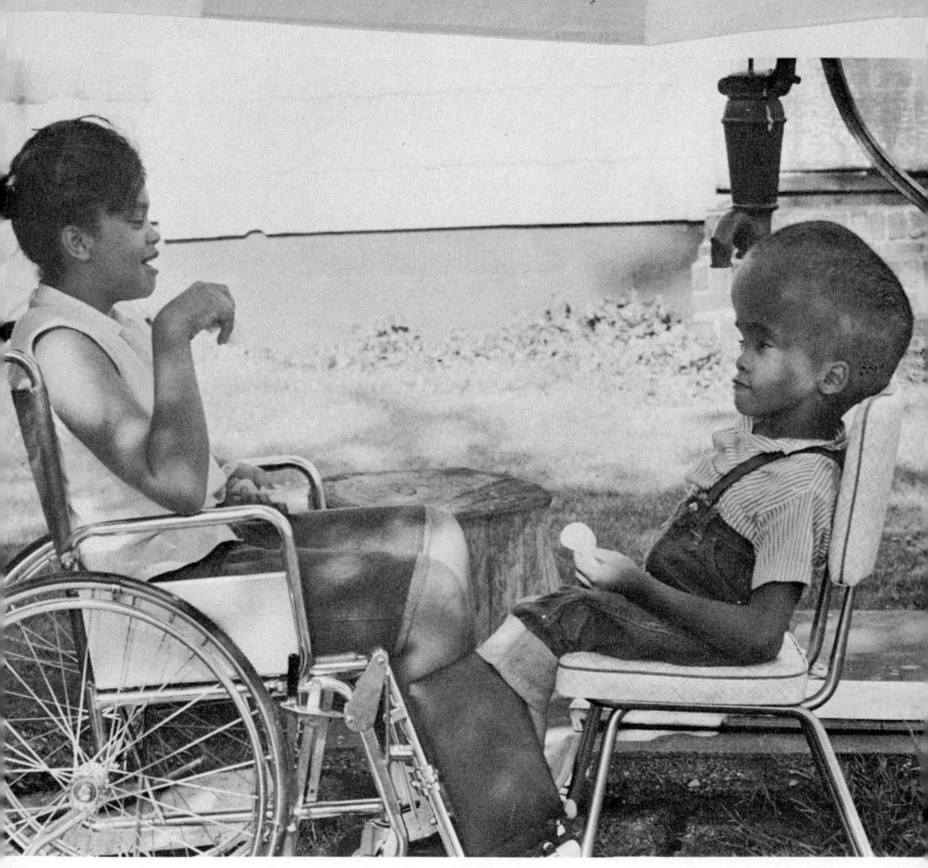

home, Junior swaps places with big sister, Karen

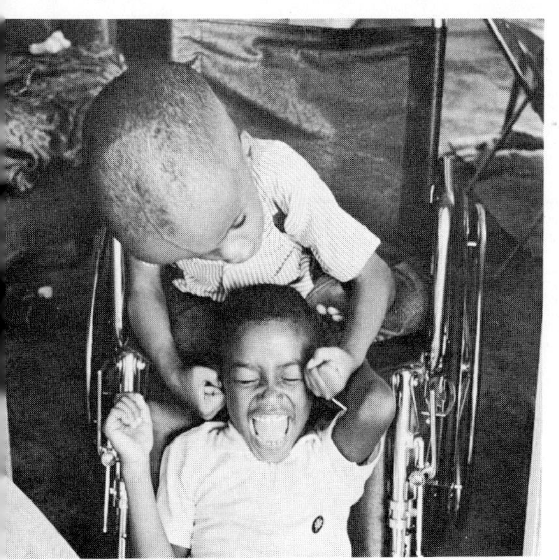

ɔck fights with his brother, Steve,

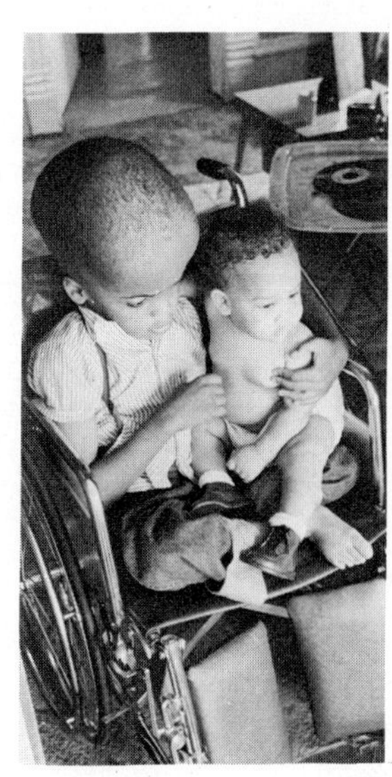

and cuddles baby
brother, Brian

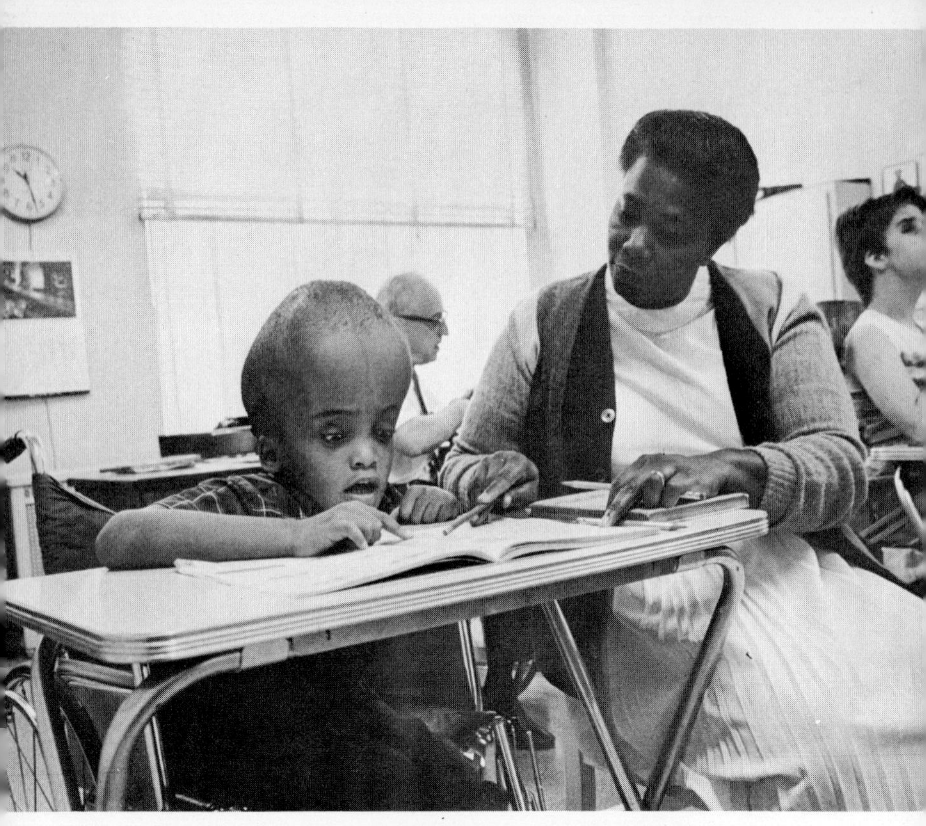

Learning at the Illinois Hospital School through study

and pla

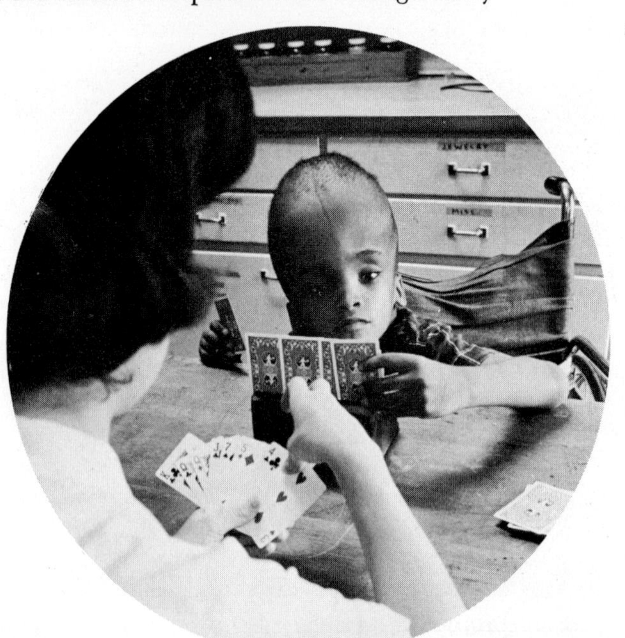

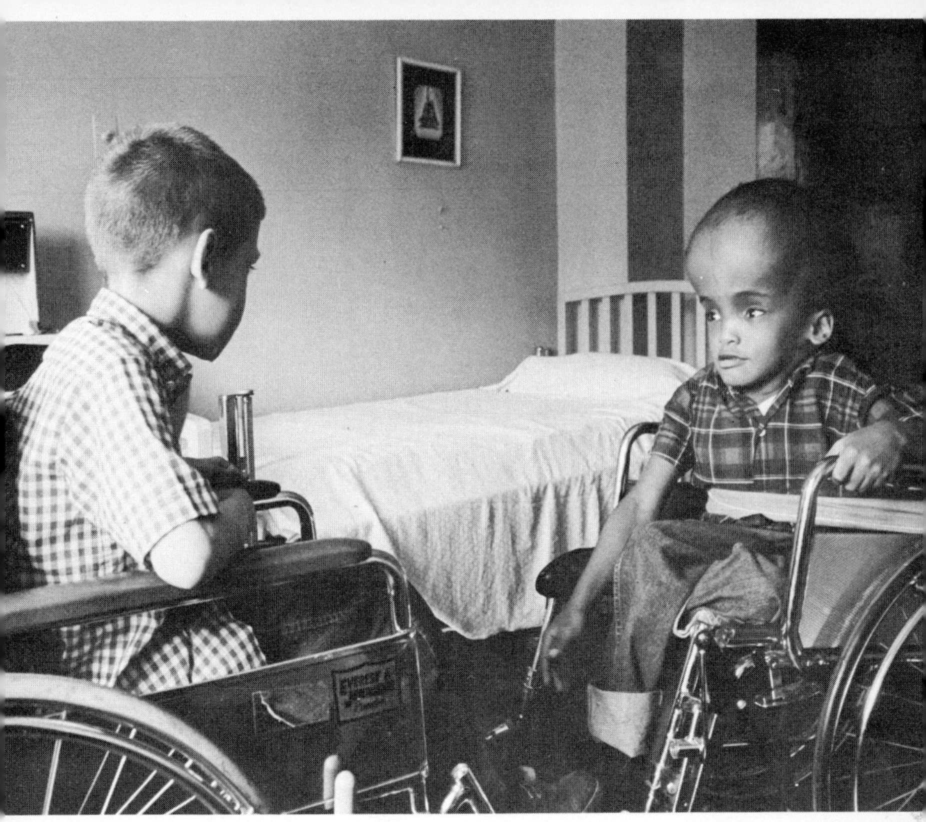

unior has a roommate

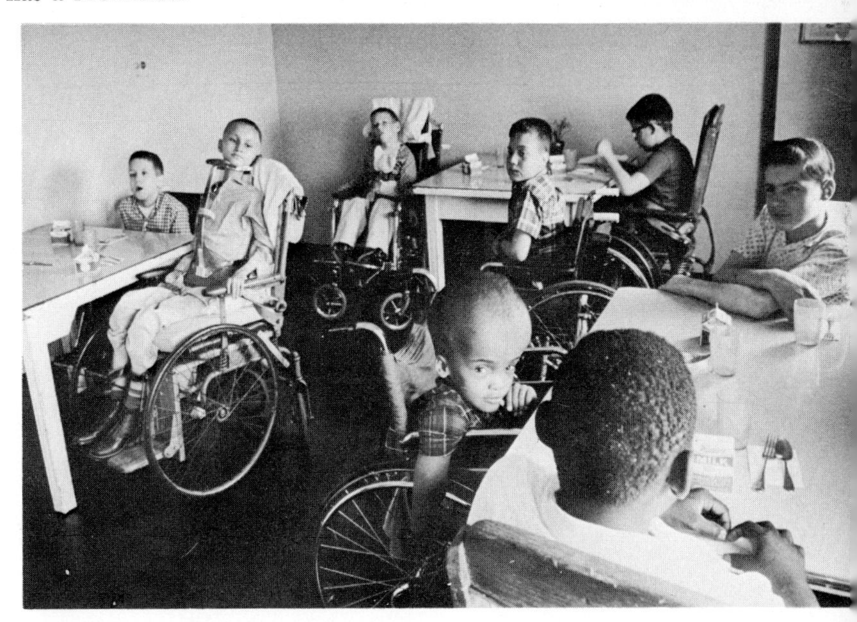

and also socializes, after school hours, with other children on his floor.

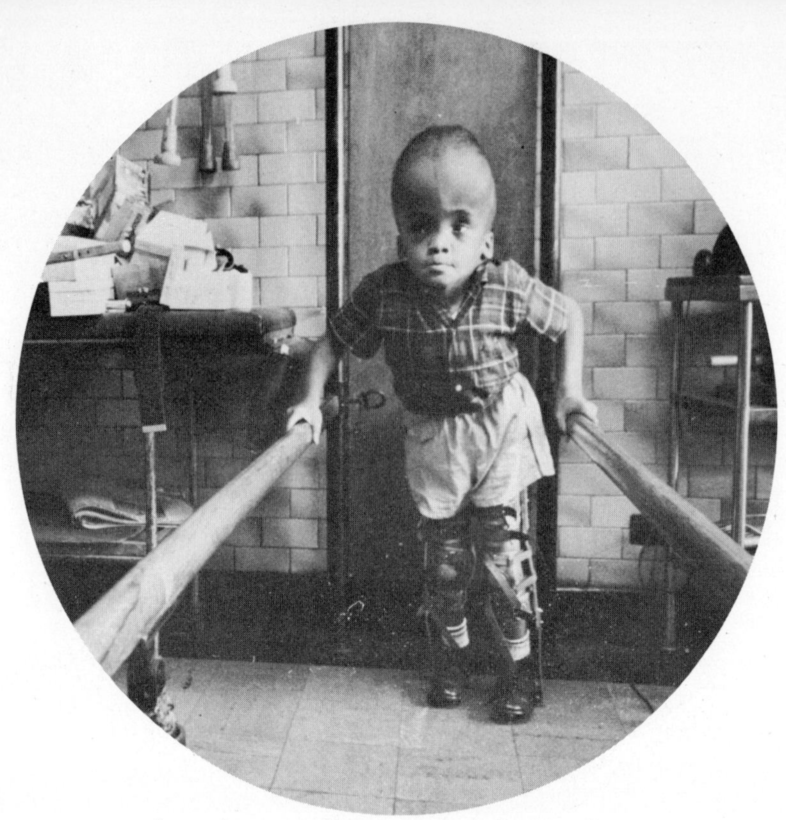

Learning to walk in physical therapy classes

and with his parents.

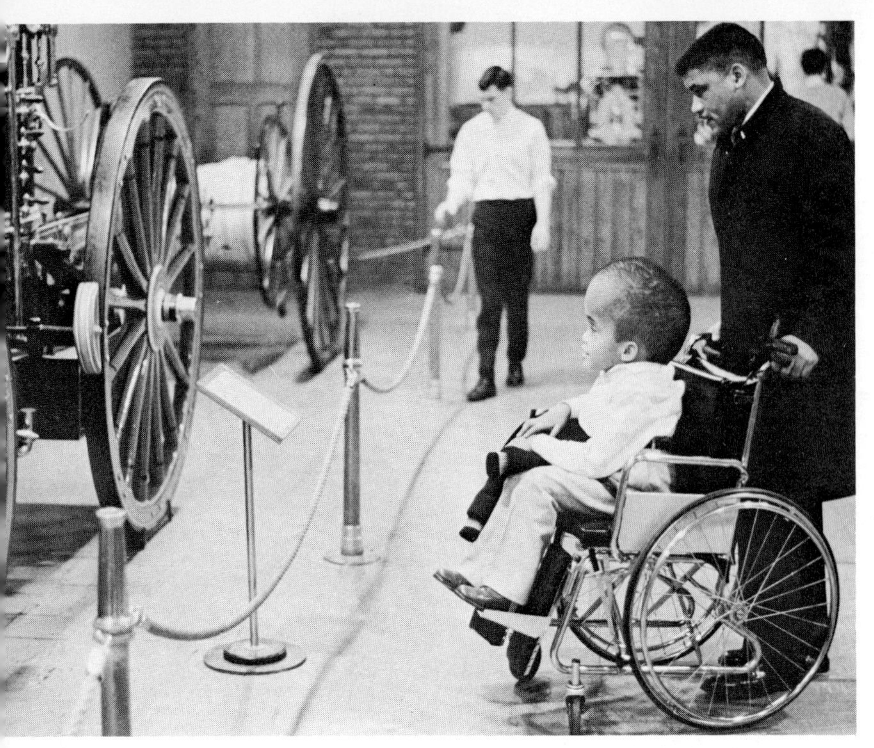

nior visits the Museum of Science and Industry with his father

DEAR MOTHER
I LOVE YOU VERY
HAPPY MOTHERS
DAY 6479119

Delbret Pattneson

and writes home on mother's day.

Progress report—to April, 1965

Last report

STATE OF ILLINOIS
DEPARTMENT OF CHILDREN AND FAMILY SERVICES
ILLINOIS CHILDREN'S HOSPITAL-SCHOOL
Richard Eddy, Superintendent

April 2, 1965
Date

Dear Parents:

Delbert Patterson has been in the Hospital-School program for 1 years and 1 months.
He/She has made satisfactory progress at his achievement levels as indicated:

Arithmetic	E–	at	2nd	grade level
English	C+	at	2nd	grade level
Reading	C	at	2nd	grade level
Spelling	B–	at	2nd	grade level

He/She has been doing work in other subject areas with his group:

Social Studies	
Science	B
Art	
Music	

A-Excellent, B-Above Average, C-Average, D-Below Average, and U-Unsatisfactory

Teacher's Comment: Delbert continues to make steady gains in school. He has shown slight improvement in his conduct since last marking period.

Paul A. Kavanaugh
Director of Education

Marion H. Chandler
Teacher

Junior was able to spend his summer vacation at home in 1965, and to start the new school year in the third grade.

The Patterson family together

Mrs. Givens, Katheryn Patterson's mother, helps Brian with the record player; Katheryn, Karen, and Stephen share the foreground with Delberts, Junior and Senior.

PART III

Life With Junior

DELBERT, JUNIOR

I WAS THANKFUL to be free from epileptic seizures in my second pregnancy, but I was not to get through it without some unpleasant complications. In the first two weeks I started to have pains in my chest, and these pains became increasingly severe. This discomfort didn't prevent me, however, from wanting to go on a day's trip with the women's club I belonged to. Against Pat's advice, toward the end of the second month of pregnancy, I was scrambling and climbing in Starved Rock State Park, when I had a bad fall which made me feel so ill that I had to be taken back to Chicago.

As soon as I was safely back home I called my doctor and told him what had happened. He said that I should take it easy for a couple of days, and then go in for a checkup if the pain persisted. Mom was staying with us, so it was easy for me to rest, and the sharp pain did subside, although there was still a persistent ache.

Soon I thought I was sufficiently recovered not to worry any more, and when Pat's brother Henry and his wife Marjorie gave a shower at their house for a member of the club who was soon to be married, I remembered the disappointment I had felt about my own shower and made a special effort to go. This turned out to be a mistake for very soon after I arrived and had found a seat, I felt a stabbing pain in my chest, and doubled over choking and gasping for breath. Henry rushed me to the Chicago Lying-In Hospital where, after many tests, it was discovered to be not a miscarriage but a blood clot on my left lung.

For five days, in Billings Hospital where I had been transferred, I was in a semiconscious state. To prevent the blood from clotting, an anticoagulant drug was given me. The internist told us that there was a chance that this could cause birth defects in the child I was carrying, but at the time there was no choice but to use the drug if my life was to be saved. There is no way to be sure whether or not the baby was affected; at that time, if I had died, the two-month-old foetus would have died with me, so there is no profit in thinking about what might or might not have been the cause.

After twenty-one days in hospital I was released, but for the remainder of my pregnancy I had to go into the hospital every week for a blood test, after which the dosage of the drug was adjusted.

On Good Friday, March 30th, 1956, Delbert Patterson,

Jr. was born. He was eight pounds, six and a half ounces, and he seemed to us to be the most perfect baby in the world. I had been able to watch his birth because I had been given a spinal anesthetic; labor was much easier than it had been with Karen, and for the first time I was able to experience the miracle of giving birth. Our family was growing just the way we wanted. We had our daughter, and now Delbert Junior was the son for whom we had hoped and prayed.

We were too happy to have any time for any forebodings. Even when the pediatrician asked me if large heads ran in my family, when Junior was only eight days old, I felt no apprehension. When we took the baby home our only fear, that Karen might be jealous, vanished. Karen loved and mothered Junior from the moment she saw him. All our friends and relatives came to see the baby during the next month, and everyone remarked on his big head, thinking it was a sign that he would grow to be a big man. Pat's family was especially pleased we had a son, because neither of his brothers had any children. For these few weeks we lived in happy ignorance.

HYDROCEPHALY

BY THE TIME we took Junior to the hospital for his first check-up I was beginning to worry because I had noticed that he could not turn his head from side to side while lying on his stomach. The pediatrician was concerned because Junior's head had increased in size since birth and referred us to the chief of neurology at Billings Hospital. He told us that we should take the baby into Bobs Roberts Hospital when he was eight weeks old and reluctantly, with growing apprehension, we did so. Little Junior went through so much in such a short time. It was heartbreaking to see his shaven head, punctured with the needles that had been inserted in an attempt to drain the fluid from his brain. For the first time I could not avoid seeing that his head was abnormally large.

Then came the day when I was summoned to the hospital to hear the explanation of our son's condition, when I had to tell Pat that Junior was a hydrocephalic who, if he survived at all, would probably be a helpless imbecile. With no real hope, Pat and I returned to the hospital the next day and saw the neurosurgeon, who could only repeat what I had already learned. There was nothing further that could be done for Junior. The doctor added that we should think about finding an institution for handicapped children where Junior could be cared for.

He went on: "As his head grows you will not be able to handle him, and if by some miracle he lives, he will not be able to do anything for himself. He is hydrocephalic. There has been extensive brain damage. If he lives he will be an imbecile."

We thanked the doctor and went back to see Junior. As I looked down on the helpless baby my main emotion was one of self-pity. I felt I could almost see his head growing as I looked at him, and I couldn't help being horrified at having produced a baby who was abnormal. But still, there was no doubt for either of us about what we should do. Junior was ours, and we made arrangements to take him home as soon as he could be released. Pat and I went home alone, and talked. We talked endlessly about the shame and the ridicule we would have to face, about the ordeal of taking our odd-looking child out in public. We wondered what our friends and family would think. How would our daughter Karen react? Pat for the time being was quite crushed by this sudden cruel awakening from his dreams of fishing trips, baseball games, hunting excursions and father-and-son talks. He looked and acted as though fate had kicked him in the stomach. We felt guilty and ashamed, and rejected the idea that this could really be happening to us.

Then we brought Junior home. This time it was not the joyous occasion that it had been when Pat brought us home after his birth. This time we felt furtive. We wanted to hide Junior and ourselves. We were consumed with self-pity. We both wept whenever we looked at each other. For awhile I was afraid of my own baby and I had to force my-self to look at him or touch him. The baby that I had wanted so much had now become repulsive to me.

Meanwhile, Mom wasn't saying much. She had taken charge of Junior when we brought him home. She gave him the love and the cuddling and attention that I could not bring myself to give him, wallowing as I was in thoughts of myself, and in anticipating what people would think and say about me for giving birth to a deformed child. Finally, Mom sat down one day and said, "Look here child, don't you know God makes no mistakes? He gave you that baby for a purpose. Who do you think you are to question God's doing? Instead of sitting first in one chair and then in another, mooning and feeling sorry for your-self, you should be thanking Him for sparing you, and for giving that baby life."

These were not to be Mom's last words on the subject, but they were sufficiently sharp to get me to listen, and to begin to wonder if maybe she was right.

It wasn't easy. We hated taking Junior out. We detested

the stares. Strangers would actually stand and stare at him with their mouths open. They seemed quite unashamed as they whispered and pointed. But Mom insisted that the situation be met head on. So we took Junior everywhere we went.

Mom didn't have an easy job trying to convince us that we should have faith. But in her slow, self-assured way, she kept talking to us—and she continued to pray for us. Mom was slow to move, slow to speak and slow to anger. When old clothes wore out, she would piece quilts with them. She appreciated all of God's gifts, and she said God didn't like waste. I know she felt that Junior had his place in our lives, but every day when we took him out I was reliving my own experiences as an epileptic and suffering from every suspected stare or comment. The stares and whispers awaited us every time we went outside the house. And Junior's head was still growing fast.

After a time, however, Mom's philosophy prevailed. We began to look at Junior as a human being, with feelings of his own. When he began to recognize the members of the family he smiled at us affectionately and easily. Junior convinced us that he was lovable, and we found that we really did love him. He was a sweet child, and as we began to accept him for himself a new life unfolded before us. Our family became closer. Junior's birth was like cement to our marriage and to our love. Our marriage had had a shaky beginning but now we felt tightly bound together, with no room in our lives for blame and accusation. We decided to have another child as soon as possible, and to give our baby son all the love, devotion, and understanding he so deserved and needed.

As time went on, our own attitude made it easier for us to bear the cruelty of others. Pat, Karen and I were frequent visitors to Jackson Park Beach in Chicago. We had a new baby and we wanted to include him in our outings. Mom encouraged us to do this because she felt that we had to face this experience, even though she knew how hard it was going to be for Pat and I, and eventually for Junior. We chose a hot summer day in July. Junior was three-and-a-half months old. His head was enormous compared to his tiny body. The constant gazing began as soon as Pat lifted Junior out of the car. People walking past stopped, and directed their eyes straight to Junior's head. As we walked past others, we were pointed at. We walked on with heads high, jaws tight, and hearts aching. We kept going until we found a nice shady spot. By the time we got our blanket spread out, we had attracted the attention of most people in the area. At least a dozen people paraded back and forth, pointing and snickering. We stuck it out, but it did unnerve us, and it demanded a new determination in controlling our emotions. We knew we had to learn to keep our inner feelings to ourselves.

Controlling his temper was specially difficult for Pat because he carried the target (Junior) all the time when we went out.

On one occasion Pat decided to give me a change of routine by taking me out to dinner. Mom was gone home for the week-end, so he had to go to Altgeld Gardens for the babysitter. As usual he took Karen and Junior with him. As he was coming down the walk, a man standing in a second floor window called to someone in the rear "Hey come look at this." Pat looked up and saw a man pointing at Junior. Pat tensed, but walked on across the courtyard, his legs feeling like lead. Just as he was reaching the door he heard a woman call across to a friend, "Look out the window at the big head on that baby!"

At that moment Pat could have murdered anybody and everybody in sight. That kind of universal anger passes quickly, though not easily. There has not been a month in Junior's life when someone has not stared, pointed, or whispered about him. It has become easier for us to endure these cruelties as we have become used to them, and have learned to think of them as the product of carelessness or ignorance. But we can never be indifferent to seeing Junior subjected to such inhumanity.

JUNIOR AND THE FAMILY

WHEN JUNIOR was three months old I returned to work. Mom took care of the children during the week, going home at weekends, and I tried to earn some money to pay off our hospital expenses. It was during this period that Junior first began to move. He loved to lie and listen to the radio, and one day Mom noticed that he was wriggling from one side of the bed to the other. She stopped and watched him; to the tune of "Blue Suede Shoes," sung by Elvis Presley, our baby was doing his own version of the Twist, and laughing with pleasure. Mom's religion frowned on dancing and on secular music, but this didn't stop her from buying the Presley record. Junior loved it. He began to keep time to the music, wiggling from head to toe as he was lying flat on his back, and Mom would pretend to dance with him, even though she had no sense of rhythm.

Mom also began to read to Junior from the Bible—perhaps in order to counter the jazz influence. He enjoyed their daily readings; we started to buy more books and records for him; and he continued to improve. As Junior responded more to attention Pat played with him a lot, and they would sing and laugh together for hours.

Though it was to be a long time before Junior would be able to move, and then only in a very limited way (he is only now, at the age of 9, beginning to learn to walk), he developed in other ways like a normal child. He talked at about the same age as the other children, and was mentally alert and responsive to attention very early.

In the Spring of 1957 we left Chicago, and moved to Robbins, Illinois. My mother's sister, Mary Johnson, found an apartment for us, and we were very happy to be able to move out of the city again. I soon became pregnant again, and since I felt ill for nearly all of the nine months, it was very fortunate that I had so many of my family nearby. Mom took Junior to Centralia with her for a time, and Karen started kindergarten.

Eventually my labor pains started, and I realized one of the disadvantages of living in the country. I was a long way away from the hospital, and I had to ask our landlord, Mr. Stanly, to drive me into the city. We did reach the hospital in plenty of time, but my pains were only five minutes apart as we left Robbins, and I am sure Mr. Stanly was more nervous than I was. It was his first experience of this kind. For me, it was my first experience of an easy birth. Only a few hours after reaching the hospital a healthy baby boy of seven pounds, thirteen ounces was born. I was overjoyed, and Pat was so proud I believe he could have kissed the doctor. He kissed me instead.

When we took Stephen Merrell Patterson home, a new chapter opened for us all, and especially for Junior. We called our second son after a Christian saint and martyr, perhaps because we hoped he would perform miracles, and added the family name of Merrell because we wanted him to have the name of his father, his brother Delbert, and his grandmother, Isabelle Merrell. Stevie has been a wonderful and faithful friend to Junior. As he has developed and learned in the way of a normal child, Junior has been inspired to compete with him and their affection for each other has grown from the moment we brought Stevie home and put him into Junior's arms as he lay on our bed.

Soon after Stephen's birth we moved again. Our apartment was too small for our larger family and a friend of ours, Mrs. Dorothy Clark, suggested that we share a large house which she and her husband had bought in Morgan Park, a Chicago suburb. We accepted gladly. It was only two blocks from school, and though it was a return to Chicago there was a lovely back yard for the children to play in, and it would not be city life.

It was here, when Junior was in his third year, that things really began to happen. One night, Pat and I heard a grunting sound from the children's room. When we jumped up and ran in to see what was happening we saw Mom, on her knees praying, and Junior on his stomach on the floor, trying hard to push up. Every night, from this time on, we would hear this grunting sound as Junior fought to raise himself. About a month later, as Junior and Stevie and I were watching television, I saw Junior lift his head from the floor. I was terrified because I felt sure he must have broken his neck. I screamed, Pat came running, and both babies started to cry, but Junior dropped his head back down again, unharmed.

My first thought was to telephone Mom in Centralia, although I was shaking so with excitement that my fingers fumbled the dial. When I got through and told her the wonderful news, Mom said, "Thank God. I knew my baby would be all right."

For some weeks afterwards we all watched Junior closely, and about a month later he lifted his head again. From that time on we knew that he would indeed be "all right."

While Karen mothered and charmed the two babies, they began seriously to compete with each other. When Junior noticed Stevie trying to sit up, he would push him over. When he couldn't prevent him, he began to hold his head up more often and more strongly. Then Stevie started learning to walk, and Junior would pull his legs out from under him. As Stevie learned to move pretty fast, this method no longer worked, so Junior started to roll over and over to keep up. Soon Junior could roll faster than Stevie could crawl.

So in December 1958, when we took Junior to the hospital for what was to be his final examination by a staff of neurosurgeons we had a surprise for them. They were amazed at the progress he had made in the two years since they had seen him. He could now hold up his head while lying on his stomach, and while the doctors digested this shock Junior said to them "Want to play cards, Doc?" I shall never forget the expressions on their faces. In some way, they told us, the fluid had found another outlet and hydrocephalus had been arrested.

When we got home there was general rejoicing. My main emotion was of gratitude to my dear grandmother who had given us the help we had so badly needed to accept and adjust to the situation. Now we felt we had witnessed a miracle, and were full of hope for the future.

The doctor recommended that we try to get a special chair for Junior, and that we take him to a physical therapy center on Chicago's South Side. This was a disappointment and a setback to our hopes, because the therapist told us that Junior needed no physical therapy. I couldn't believe this was true, so Mom, Pat and I worked to try to strengthen Junior's leg and body muscles, though we knew nothing about physical therapy. I believe our efforts did help him, and now, at the Illinois Children's Hospital School, he has therapy every day and gets progressively stronger. His tiny feet have grown, his legs are stronger, and a walker has been ordered for him.

Just before Christmas of that year, Mom decided to go home for a few days. She and Pop were to come back and spend Christmas with us. On December 22nd I talked with her on the telephone. I had some good news for her—Junior had been measured for his special chair—but it was very difficult for me to understand her. Her normally soft voice was harsh, and if I had not been sure it was Mom, I would have thought I was talking to a stranger. She wanted to do all the talking. There were things she wanted to say, and she seemed not to have time to listen to me. She told me that if she didn't make it to Chicago for Christmas I was to be sure and make it a good one for the children. She told me to remember her in my prayers. That was the last time I heard her voice. No one knew that Mom was sick. On December 23rd, 1958, she died.

It was Mom who had shown us how to accept and then to love and enjoy Junior, and Pat and I had become dependent on her quiet strength as a part of our lives. We missed her sadly, but her effect on our lives was permanent. She had given Junior her strength and her courage and she had shown us what faith could do.

The special chair (a gift of the Illinois Easter Seal Society) that Mom had wanted so much for Junior meant that soon he was able to sit up, and to eat meals with the rest of the family. He had already learned to feed himself while lying on the floor, and with his head and body supported by the chair, he soon learned to eat normally. His digestive system took a little time to adjust to the new position, and at first he was nauseated when he ate, but soon this passed. All the time Junior was becoming more able to live normally with his family, and every step he made was a new source of satisfaction and joy to us.

WE LEAVE THE CITY

IN THE EARLY SPRING of 1959 Pat and I decided to leave Chicago. Since Mom's death, most of my salary had gone to baby-sitters and for transportation to work. Neither of us was really happy in the city, and we felt that as Junior grew up he would be subjected to less hostility and unkind curiosity away from the city environment. We both left our jobs, and went back to Centralia where Pop, living alone now, and incapacitated by arthritis, welcomed our company.

For six months we lived from day to day. Pat could not get a full-time job in Centralia and I could not get any kind of job. I had two babies in diapers and an invalid grandfather to take care of, and I was always tired. But we were happy. Centralia looked different to me now; the people were nicer; my children were accepted. Pat and I joined a social club, and made a lot of friends. The children, especially Junior, enjoyed the family socializing that became a large part of our lives, and people were good to him, which erased much of the bitterness I had felt toward my home town. Another scar that was finally healed was my high school graduation. I took advantage of our move back to Centralia to return to C.T.H.S. and receive my diploma. It was a good feeling to have removed myself from the nation's drop-outs! Centralia was now my home, and I was happy to be there.

Returning to my childhood home with a fresh viewpoint seemed also to give me a better understanding of my father. His lack of affection to me when I was a young girl now seemed less incomprehensible, and he proved to be a very loving grandfather, visiting the children whenever he was in town. We began to build a new relationship on our better understanding of each other, and of course this increased my happiness.

For a time after we moved to Centralia Pat stayed in his job in Chicago, driving to and from Centralia, so we were separated for much longer than ever before in our married life. During this time I became ill, and once, while hanging out clothes in the back yard, fell into an unconscious state which my doctor thought might have been caused by tension. I was in hospital for a time, and my father came to visit me every day, which made me feel even more secure in our new relationship. He told me once that I should always take care of Mother, and never mistreat her. This evidence of his having still a deep feeling for Mother, even though he had remarried, must also have helped to heal some of the emotional wounds that I had suffered in my childhood in Centralia.

When Pat quit his Chicago job and found work in Centralia, my health improved, but the new relationship with my father did not have a chance to mature. On October 18th, 1959, Dad was killed, with his wife, in an automobile accident. Mother offered to come to Centralia a week before the funeral, but I thought it better that she should not. I remembered Dad's asking me to take care of her, and I didn't want her to experience the coldness of his family, which was already being hurtful enough to me.

After Dad's death we began planning to move again. Pat found a job in the foundry at International Harvester Company in Canton, Illinois, and we moved to Dunfermline, a little town near Canton.

We were reluctant to leave Pops, but he promised to move in with us before the end of the year. There had been so much happening about this time that I had not noticed Junior's progress in about a week. In these last weeks in Centralia he began to pull himself along with his arms, instead of crawling. Stevie was mobile enough to explore on his own, so this had left Pops and Junior to enjoy each other's company for a time. They would sing and pray together all day long. People in the neighborhood began to call Junior "Deacon" and Pat and I said he would be the first dancing preacher in the history of the Baptist Church. Our concern about the attitude of other children and adults was beginning to disappear; it is a shock when people first see Junior, because of the great size of his head, but his personality is so charming and his smile so warm that he very soon wins their hearts.

After one month in Dunfermline, with our furniture moved and arranged in our new home and Karen started at school, Pat was laid off. He found work at a garage, but it didn't pay much and didn't last long. The lay-off lasted for ten months and then Pat was called back to work, but only for two months. For the first time in our lives we went on relief. I had to go to work as a cleaning woman. We found the situation degrading, but we had small children and had no choice. Seeing the children happy made things easier for us.

The children were quite a handful at this time. Junior was five years old, but I hadn't been able to toilet train him because of a partial paralysis. So I had two babies in diapers. I had tried to train Junior when he was two, and I could tell that he understood what I wanted him to do, but just wasn't able to summon the necessary control. I watched him and noticed that he was never aware of urinating or having a bowel movement. This worried me, so I took Junior to the doctor for a check-up, and he explained that the muscles from the waist down were underdeveloped, which meant that sometimes he had feeling and sometimes he didn't. The attempt to toilet train him then had to be abandoned, but on the advice of the public health nurse in Canton I took Junior to the Elks Crippled Children's Clinic. Through them he started to have physical therapy treatments once a week at home, and this cured his partial paralysis. After that, he soon learned control.

We lived in a two-story house in Dunfermline, and it didn't take Junior long to learn how to negotiate the steps on his own. One evening Pat and I were standing at the front door and were horrified to hear a series of loud bumps from the stairs. We ran inside and reached the bottom of the stairs at the same time as Junior, who was unconscious, limp, and blue. Pat snatched him up and we rushed him to Graham Hospital. By the time the doctor arrived Junior, still unconscious, was vomiting continuously, and Pat and I were terrified. We were afraid that we were losing him, and all that night, while Pat went back to Dunfermline to be with Karen and Stevie, I sat by his crib. He vomited until his stomach was empty, and gagged for the rest of the night. I talked to him, and prayed, but he showed no sign of response.

The next morning Pat came in, and I went home to change my clothes. When I reached the hospital again Pat had the X-ray report from the doctors. Junior had four fractures in his head. For four days he couldn't talk to us, but on the Wednesday after his fall he recovered consciousness and the doctors told us he was going to be all right.

The nurses and patients on his floor did not know he was an alert hydrocephalic, but as soon as he was well enough to talk they found out. As usual, he charmed everybody around him. He was in the hospital for ten days, and made a complete recovery.

In the July of 1960 Pops, my grandfather, came to live

with us in Dunfermline. He had been taken ill in Centralia, and when he was released from the hospital Pat and I, Mother and her husband Reginald Givens, and Aunt Mary and her husband all drove to Centralia to ask him which of us he would like to stay with. Pat and I were very happy that he chose us, and we knew that Junior would be delighted to have his companionship again. The day after we brought him to Dunfermline, however, Pops became violently ill and we took him to the Graham Hospital in Canton, where it was discovered that he had diabetes. From that time on, Pops had to have regular insulin injections, which I learned to give him. At first I was nervous and clumsy, but Pat was unable to bring himself to do it at all!

Pops was always good-natured, and though he was almost completely bed-ridden he was wonderful company for me and the children at a time when we still didn't know many people in the neighborhood. First thing in the morning Junior would always join Pops in bed; they would have their "prayer meeting" together, and often Junior would be with him most of the day. Unfortunately this happy period only lasted for three months. In late October Pops died as the result of a cerebral hemorrhage, and it was a lonely house without him. Junior looked for him every morning for some time, and Karen and Stevie did their best to help him to get used to the idea of Pops' absence.

We have taught the other children to love and respect Junior as an individual. He is not forced on them, but they include him in their everyday activities out of love and habit. Through Karen, Junior has learned some of the things she has learned in school which were advanced for a normal child, and unheard of in a hydrocephalic. With Stevie he has learned how to share his play activities and cooperate with other children. Junior has been taught to accept the fact that there are some things he can't do, and although he'll try anything once, he doesn't fret over his failures. He finds other ways to amuse himself.

One of the lessons Junior taught me about his determination occurred when, in 1961, he had ten teeth extracted. Only three days afterwards he asked for an ear of corn. I told him that his gums were too sore, but he insisted, so I gave it to him to prove my point. He proved his instead. He took one bite, said "Ouch" and proceeded to eat the whole ear of corn without flinching.

His ability to endure discomfort and pain without complaint is remarkable; until 1962 he had a large hernia on the right side of his groin which he had had since birth. In the Spring of 1962 he was fitted with waist to ankle braces, and the hernia made these very uncomfortable to wear. So in July the hernia was removed by surgery and he was in the hospital for a week. The nurses told me that sometimes when they went into his room they would find tears streaming down his cheeks because of the pain he was in, but he never cried out or complained. As usual when in hospital, he was a good patient and endeared himself to everyone who came in contact with him.

SCHOOL FOR JUNIOR

WHEN JUNIOR WAS FIVE, I started a classroom in his room at home. At that time we didn't have any hope that he would be able to go to school, so I wrote to Mrs. Laura Tate, the kindergarten teacher at Lincoln School in Centralia, asking her for advice and help in how to go about teaching a child a kindergarten curriculum. Mrs. Tate was very helpful, sending me enough mimeographed material to last for a year. We had a regular kindergarten routine. Junior loved school, and infected Stevie with the same spirit of enjoyment.

After a couple of months working with Junior I could see how much he was learning. He was so eager to learn, and eager to please. One day the public health nurse, Mrs. Wilma Sturgeon, was visiting and she noticed how alert he was, and particularly how well he could speak. Mrs. Sturgeon suggested that I take him to the Institute of Juvenile Research at Peoria, where the psychologist who tested him was pleased with the results. He scored slightly below his age level because his attention span—his ability to stick to one project for long—was limited, but he was educable. I was told to take Junior back to the Institute in a year's time, when it could be decided how we could best get him started on an education.

I continued to work with Junior at home. His progress was good, and I concentrated more on increasing his attention span than on academic instruction, and this brought a gratifying improvement.

Finally, in 1962, we began our fight for Junior's right to an education. We decided that we would once again move back to Centralia. I had mixed feelings about the idea, but we felt that Centralia had the best educational system. Most of the teachers there had taught me, knew me and my family, and I had a lot of respect for them.

On September 5th, 1962, I took Junior in for an appointment with the special education teacher and the principal of my home town school. Once again he took an intelligence test, which he passed. He also came through an oral interview without difficulty. The only impediment to his admission to school was his inability to walk, but this proved to be insurmountable. He could not gain admission to the Lincoln School because they felt it would be too much of a risk. This was a bad setback to our plans because we felt that if this school, which was a new buildnig, all on one floor, could not take the responsibility of accepting our son, his prospects elsewhere were very bad. We felt that the real reason for Junior's rejection was his appearance, and the way he used his elbows to pull himself along. Although this unusual way of crawling looked odd at first sight, it worked very well. Junior could have participated in normal classroom activities, and had been properly trained to take care of himself in the washroom.

We had been so sure that Junior would be accepted by the Lincoln School that we had already registered Karen in the fourth grade. Deeply discouraged, we collected the children, taking Karen out of school after only a day and a half, and headed back to Canton.

The struggle continued in Canton. I had been informed by the city superintendent of schools there that the public schools system would accept him, so I went along to the Kellogg Kindergarten to find out if he should attend morning or afternoon school. Here I met with the news that he could not be admitted, on the orders of the city superintendent.

Junior had been looking forward to school for almost a year. He had endured many intelligence tests and had shown that he was educable. His disappointment was as keen as our own and, as a family, we were determined to fight back.

We did not live near a city with a school for physically handicapped children; we learned that there were several non-ambulatory students in Canton's public schools; we knew that there was nothing in the Illinois School Code that would justify the schools system in refusing Junior an education. I felt that my son was being denied one of his basic rights, and I notified a national magazine of our dilemma. One phone call to the city superintendent opened the way for Junior to be tested yet again. We resented this on our son's behalf, and he was disgusted, but he passed and in the second week of September he started to attend kindergarten in public school.

Junior adjusted beautifully to kindergarten. His first teacher, Mrs. Noe, explained Junior's condition to the children before Pat took him in on his first day, and they accepted him naturally and easily. He made friends quickly, and none of the children were upset by the way he crawled or by the sight of his large head.

After three months, Junior developed a kidney infection, and we took him out of school. The experience had been very good for him, but it is an old school, with the kindergarten housed in the basement of the building, and the bare concrete floors in the washroom, where Junior crawled and changed clothes, seemed to us to be something to which we should not expose him again. I taught him at home for the rest of the school year.

Junior's time in public school had opened up other possibilities. He had been interviewed by a member of the admitting board of one of the state's best schools for the educable physically handicapped. The superintendent of schools had taken a real interest in Junior after he saw how concerned we were about his education, and it was suggested that we apply for admission at the Illinois Children's Hospital School in Chicago.

We hated the thought of Junior going away to school, but if he were accepted there would be a much increased chance for his rehabilitation. With more frequent physical therapy, he might be able to learn to walk, and the education he could get, right up to high school graduation, would be a good one. The application was made, and in the Spring of 1963 he was accepted and his name put on the long waiting list. In the months when Junior was waiting to start school he was very lucky to have the help of Mrs. Settles, a homebound special education state teacher. She worked with him every morning, five days a week, preparing him to enter first grade at the Hospital School, and was especially responsible for improving his understanding of numbers and ability to work with them. Her training is still an asset to him. Junior still thinks of her as "his teacher," and she is the first person he calls when he comes home.

The summer of 1963 passed slowly. We were waiting to learn if Junior could start school in September, and I was expecting our fourth child. Junior was impatient to see the new baby; he came into my room every morning to ask "Is the baby here yet?" When we heard that Junior would not be starting school that September we were relieved, because we had not wanted him to miss the arrival of the baby he had looked forward to for so long.

Brian Tracy (as he was named by Karen) arrived on September 28th, 1963. Pat took me into the hospital at

2 in the morning, but Karen assured me there was no need to worry about things at home. She would take care of the boys. "If daddy isn't back in time for breakfast, I will fix it." Karen was only ten, but during the time I was away she took care of the housework and the cooking, dressed Stevie for kindergarten every day, and even had hot coffee waiting for Pat when he came home from work at 7 in the morning. Both the boys behaved themselves, and gave her little trouble. Pat and I were so proud of our children, and so happy when we brought Brian home and saw their excitement and joy at having the family together again. Junior loved the baby as soon as he saw him, and tells everyone that Brian is *his* baby.

That year we planned to have an especially good Christmas as a reward to the children. Our best efforts were well rewarded on Christmas Day as our family eagerly opened their gifts, and Brian lay placidly enjoying the Christmas tree lights. Pat and I looked at each other and knew how fortunate we were.

CHICAGO HOSPITAL SCHOOL

We heard in February, 1964, that Junior could be admitted to the Illinois Children's Hospital School. We had waited a long time for this news, and we genuinely felt that it would open new horizons for Junior, but of course our emotions were mixed. For purely selfish reasons, we were reluctant to let him go. Junior had become the center of our family, and we realized, as we faced the prospect of sending him off to a life which would release him to us for only a few weeks in the year, that his absence would leave a painful gap in our lives. The eight years since his birth had entirely wiped out the horror and despair that we had felt when we learned of Junior's illness when he was a tiny baby.

I feel that our happiness together speaks for itself in answering those people who told us that we should not have tried the experiment of keeping Junior with us. And even those who, with greater understanding, have told us that we should be commended for bringing him up at home, have missed the point. We have gained far more from having Junior with us than we have given him. He has knitted us more closely together; he has given all of us a new outlook on life; he has taught us to be more sensitive and aware of others. The two babies born after Junior have felt his delight in and love for them from their earliest moments, and they have learned so much from him that his parents could never have taught them.

As we faced the prospect of Junior's imminent departure we realized more and more his importance in our lives. He competes with Brian in the same way as he did with Stevie five years ago. When the baby learned to use a walker, Junior encouraged Brian to chase him in his wheel chair. They squeal and laugh so hard when they are playing together it sounds like an army of children. Sometimes, especially when Junior is trying to play the record player, Brian will get in his hair by climbing all over him. It would warm anyone's heart to see them together.

Junior's love of music has had its special effect on our household, too. He has always loved to dance, and he has developed his sense of timing along with a genuine appreciation of music. No matter what the current dance craze is, Junior finds a way to do it. One night, Pat and I were playing Sam Cooke's recording of "Twisting the Night Away" when we heard the bed moving in the boys' room. Pat looked in on them and saw Junior doing the twist, fast asleep. Pat put him on the floor, and he twisted through the entire record without opening his eyes; when it ended, Pat put him back in bed, still sound asleep.

Another of Junior's delights is singing; he sings along with Mahalia Jackson, closing his eyes, and losing himself in the music. His particular favorite is "You'll Never Walk Alone"—and for a nine-year-old boy he sings well. His voice is good, like his father's who loves to sing and is an enthusiastic choir member.

One of his latest exploits occurred when he was sitting in his wheel chair, which was standing next to our car. The car radio was on and when a record with the right beat was played Junior started doing "the monkey" in his chair. Pat called me, and we watched him through to the end, never missing a beat.

Junior will accept no limitations on what he will try to do, at least once. His hobby, believe it or not, is baseball. After he had been in school a couple of months he asked for a baseball glove and he has learned how to use it. He has a good eye for throwing—either from his wheel chair, or lying down. He can also bat from either position. We tried telling him gently that he probably never will be able to play in a baseball game, but his mind is made up. He says he will play if he has to lie on the ground to do it!

Junior's acceptance by the hospital school was the culmination of our long search for a way for him to receive an education in line with his intelligence, and of the efforts and help we had received from other people. Among all these, Miss Frances James, a public health nurse, was the most important. She had been instrumental in getting

Junior a specially built walker; she had worked with Dr. Stuttle of the Elks Crippled Children's Clinic to get Junior the waist to ankle braces which have made it possible for him to stand; she interested two sororities and the Y-Teens of Canton to make contributions to get him a wheel chair as a going away present when he left for the hospital school. Our debt of gratitude to her is more than can ever be put into words.

And so, on March 17th, 1964, Pat and I went with Junior to the Illinois Children's Hospital and saw him start out on the road to a better life. We spent the whole day there, and were deeply impressed.

We were welcomed by the school superintendent, Mr. Eddy, who was reassuringly friendly. All the staff that we met seemed human, and we felt a glow of warmth about them and their attitude to the children in their care. We talked for a long time to Mrs. Hicks, the social worker to whom Junior was assigned. She is a most devoted person; in the year that she has been working with Junior, she has made us feel that to her and to the Hospital School as a whole, his progress is as important as it is to us.

The School itself aims at bringing every possible service into use to help the children to an education which will fit them for a return to normal life. All the children admitted are educable, but so severely handicapped that their needs cannot be met in ordinary schools. The aim is to achieve physical rehabilitation to the greatest possible degree. The children are educated to suit their individual capabilities, and allowed to progress at their natural pace. Through living together with other children of the same age and stage of development, and in mixing with older and younger children in play and organized recreation, their social development is encouraged. Junior is getting a better education than would be possible for him in a local school, and he can carry through to high-school graduation at the Hospital School. I attended a graduation ceremony there in 1964, and it was a wonderful occasion for the children and the parents. To see how much can be accomplished by young people with handicaps that might seem, at first sight, impossible to overcome is deeply encouraging to everyone involved in similar situations. The happy atmosphere of the Hospital School speaks for the wonderful job that the staff do in helping the children to adjust and to treat their disabilities as matter-of-fact problems about which something positive can be done.

The School allows frequent vacations so that parents do not lose touch with their children, and we have no feeling of being cut off from knowing and sharing in the news of Junior's progress. Regular reports are sent to us about his physical, social, and educational development; recently all of these have been good.

Our expenses for Junior include the cost of his clothes, and some of the special equipment that he needs. The cost to the state of maintaining a child in the School for one year is $9,763.42, or $26.75 per day.

Of course we were worried that Junior might have trouble in adapting to life away from home; he had never met anyone who was physically or mentally handicapped, and we had no idea how this would affect him. As usual, our worries were groundless. His personality and friendliness to the world in general have had their usual effect, and school is being a happy experience for him. He misses his family, especially the baby, but his adjustment is so good that we cannot help but be happy for him, even though the family is only really complete when he comes home for vacations.

Junior has become quite independent in his year away at school. He has made friends and he loves them. He is always eager to return after his trips home. When we take him back after a visit he doesn't want to spend long in the lobby with us, saying goodbyes. He is always eager to get back "up on five"—the fifth floor where he lives. This is just as well, since we are only able to get into Chicago—a two-hundred-mile drive from Canton—about once a month. Mother and my stepfather, who live in Chicago, have been to visit him every weekend, and have prevented him feeling too lonely. He looks forward to their visits all the more because he knows we can't come every week. My stepfather, who has been like a father to me, has been a wonderful grandfather to all the children. He is so generous, and will give the children anything they want, though of course I try to prevent them telling him their most extravagant wishes!

In school work Junior has done very well. In fact he has progressed from a low first grade to a high second grade in one year's work, and he is to be allowed to spend the whole summer —June, July, and August—at home with us. His reading level is average for his grade, and in arithmetic (a subject that was specially difficult for him at first, because of his varying ability to remember numbers), he has made good progress. When I praised him about his improvement he told me how he had managed to do so well: "Arithmetic time," he said, "is B. T. time." I asked him what he meant. He said, "Brain therapy. I've got B. T. for my head, and P. T. [physical therapy] for my legs."

When I last talked to the physical therapist I learned that in that area too Junior is doing very nicely. He can stand very well at the parallel bars, and, with the new braces that have a lock at the knee, he is able to use a walker in the physical therapy sessions, though at the moment he still goes to classes in his wheel chair. A walker is on order for him now, and soon he should be able to use it to walk to classes and to meals. This will be a great moment for him, and for us too. Recently, when we went in to the School to collect him he said to me, "One of these times when you come after me, I'm going to walk off that elevator." It seems now that with his determination, and God's help, that day is not far off.

NO TIME FOR TEARS

ONE EVENING Karen and I were talking, after the boys were in bed. I was startled when she asked me, "Mother, what would you do if I had a handicapped child?" I told her that I thought my experience would make it easier for me to help her, as Mom had helped me. But I also said that the atmosphere she had lived in with Junior, and the way she felt about him would be her biggest asset. She would not need so much comfort and reassurance as I had. "Mother will be right by your side if you need her," I said, and she gave me a big hug and kiss and said goodnight.

We realize that it is natural for people to be curious about the unusual, and we have adjusted to the attitude of strangers, even though the reaction of the outside world is sometimes very far from the acceptance that is now natural to us. Last summer (1964) Pat and I went into the Hospital

School to take Junior home for the three-week vacation. I waited in front of the school with Junior in his wheel chair while Pat was getting the car out of the parking lot across the street. I saw a man come up to him and start talking, and though he pointed at Junior I couldn't tell from Pat's face what the conversation was about. He had been asking about the School. He said "It's awful the way all those kids are crippled up coming out of there. Some of them are really messed up. Look at the head on that little boy. I think it's a shame, pitiful."

Pat said he didn't think it was a shame or pitiful. "What those children need is understanding from people like you who have been fortunate enough to be blessed with good limbs. Another reason I don't think it pitiful is that I'm that little fellow's Dad." The man changed color, and went on down the street, without saying a word.

Junior himself disarms the wrong sort of pity by asking people who are treating him to horrified stares: "Gee, do I look that bad?" We have never tried to conceal from him the fact that he is physically different from others. We have always talked frankly about his "big head" because we feel this is necessary if he is going to grow up with a healthy attitude to life. He is quite unselfconscious about his appearance, and as soon as people get to know him, it becomes unimportant to them, too.

His personality has changed, as of course it was bound to, in his year away at the Hospital School. He was determined not to be a crybaby, and he has had every help and encouragement in developing his character and personality as well as his brain. Sometimes now he is a little flip, which is something new for him, but I think it is a defense to help him over the difficult times. The important thing for us is that we have complete confidence in Junior, and complete confidence in the School to give him the best possible chance to learn and to grow up into a well-adjusted young man. The children there reflect the kindness which is bestowed on them; there is discipline, but it is used with the child's welfare in mind, and with care and justice. The long struggle to find a way to give Junior his proper chance in life is, for the moment anyway, a struggle no more, and we are truly grateful.

We are praying that with our help and love, and the care and understanding of informed people, Junior will grow up to be a happy, healthy, and useful citizen.

I was an epileptic and I am now living a full and happy life. My hydrocephalic son has made a miraculous adjustment to his handicap and has two healthy brothers and a devoted sister to help him through life. These are prayers answered; even when we did not realize it God had his hands on us. My handicapped child is my blessing. I have no time for tears.

APPENDIX

HYDROCEPHALUS: A MEDICAL DEFINITION*

You have been told by your doctor that your child has hydrocephalus. You may already have had some explanation about this condition and what it could mean to you and your child. Although you may never have heard of hydrocephalus, you may have heard the expression "water on the brain"—and that is what the word hydrocephalus means. In any case, you were not prepared for such a condition in your own child. After recovering from the first emotional shock, most parents want to know certain things—what is hydrocephalus? what causes it? what can be done about it? These are the questions we shall attempt to answer here.

What is hydrocephalus?

Hydrocephalus is a condition people have known about since times of antiquity. Records of it exist in the history

* Reprinted by permission of the School of Medicine, Loma Linda University, Los Angeles, from their pamphlet *An Introduction to Your Child Who Has Hydrocephalus.*

of medicine and mankind long before the birth of Christ. It is a condition in which the fluid that normally flows through the center spaces of the brain either is not getting out by way of the regular channels or is not being absorbed into the blood stream at the same rate at which it is produced. When this happens, the spaces in the brain called ventricles become enlarged because of the accumulation of fluid in them. With no place to go, this fluid enlarges the ventricles and compresses the brain until finally the brain tissue is destroyed. The pressure within the brain also causes the head to grow more rapidly than normal and at a rate proportional to the severity of the condition.

Hyrdocephalus may occur before the baby is born. In such a case the enlarged head may prevent delivery of the infant unless a portion of the fluid is drained by the physician at the time of delivery or a Cesarean section is performed. Usually, however, hydrocephalus is not apparent immediately at birth but may be recognizable soon thereafter. During the first few days, weeks, or months after birth the head may begin to enlarge much more rapidly than it should. When this rapid enlargement of the head is due to the accumulation of normal brain fluid within the brain, the condition is called hydrocephalus.

What is the cause of hydrocephalus?

There are many causes of hydrocephalus, some more common than others. It is easier to understand these if first we explain something about the normal formation, flow, and absorption of cerebrospinal fluid.

Within the brain itself there are four hollow spaces called ventricles. The brain fluid, or cerebrospinal fluid, is formed in each of these ventricles by a special area of blood vessels called the choroid plexus. Two fairly large lateral ventricles, one within each side of the brain, drain into a more centrally located third ventricle. This in turn drains by means of a narrow tube or duct (the aqueduct of Sylvius) into the fourth ventricle, which is situated near the underside of the brain. The cerebrospinal fluid then flows through several tiny openings in the fourth ventricle to bathe the surface of the brain and spinal cord. On the surface of the brain the fluid is absorbed into the blood stream through special areas in the walls of the large vein called sinuses. Thus the cerebrospinal fluid circulation completes a cycle.

One can think of these ventricles as a chain of lakes, each being fed by underground springs of water and each maintaining a constant size from continuous drainage by means of a narrow connecting channel to the next lake at a slightly lower level. From the lowest lake in the chain, the water passes through several narrow outlets to spread over the meadows and be reabsorbed into the ground. If the outlet or outlets of any lake were blocked off, all the lakes above that point would swell in size because of the dam downstream. If something were to interfere with the absorption of the water into the ground, there would be a rapid accumulation of water. Or the lakes could be caused to enlarge if the underground springs were to pour in more water than could be handled by the outlets.

The same sort of thing can occur to the ventricular system within the brain. When the head swells because the ventricles are distended with fluid because of an obstruction of the narrow pathways, this is called an "obstructive" type of hydrocephalus. The most common site of obstruction is in the "aqueduct of Sylvius." Probably well over 90 per cent of hydrocephalic infants have this abnormality. When all the passageways are open or communicating, but the fluid is not being absorbed on the surface of the brain as rapidly as it is being made, the disorder is called a "communicating" type of hydrocephalus. The rarest form of hydrocephalus is that in which there is an increased formation of cerebrospinal fluid in the ventricles. This condition may be caused by a tumor in the choroid plexus.

These various explanations help one understand why some cases of hydrocephalus progress less rapidly than others. The rate of progress depends on whether the obstruction to flow or absorption is complete or partial or whether a slight excess or large excess of fluid is being formed. In rare cases when an obstruction clears up spontaneously, we have an example of arrested or self-cured hydrocephalus.

What causes the obstruction?

Most cases of hydrocephalus are congenital in origin; that is to say, the abnormality is present in the unborn child. The obstruction of the aqueduct of Sylvius, for example, is most commonly due to a failure of nature to make a single tube. Nature makes instead many tiny tubes, most of which end blindly in this area and do not make their way to the fourth ventricle. Or if they do connect, they are so small that they do not allow the fluid to get out as rapidly as it should.

Most of the time there is no known reason for the various congenital malformations causing hydrocephalus, just as in most cases there is no known cause for a congenital heart malformation or a cleft lip and cleft palate deformity or other congenital anomalies. Hydrocephalus sometimes occurs in association with other congenital abnormalities. The most frequently associated abnormality is a condition in which there is an outpouching of the spinal cord or cord coverings on the back. In such cases there is often some loss of body function below this level.

Other causes of hydrocephalus are infections and tumors of the brain which may occur during childhood. In previous times infections involving the brain and brain surface (meningitis) almost invariably ended in death. Today, treatment of these conditions often results in complete recovery. Unfortunately, however, there are cases in which the severity of the condition is such that there is permanent damage even though the child lives. In these cases pressure, adhesions, or scarring may obstruct the normal flow of cerebrospinal fluid and cause hydrocephalus.

Is hydrocephalus hereditary?

It is generally felt by neurologists and those who have studied hydrocephalus extensively that it is rarely hereditary. Hydrocephalus has occurred twice in one family, but this has happened infrequently. The actual chance of such an occurrence has been estimated as between one and five in a hundred.

How common is hydrocephalus?

Although it is uncommon, hydrocephalus is not regarded as a rare condition. It is estimated to occur once in approximately every five hundred births. This means that in a large hospital several hydrocephalic infants are born each year. In the United States alone, it is estimated, there are 8,000 new cases of hydrocephalus each year. So if you are the parent of a hydrocephalic child, you are not alone.

One sees relatively few older children and adults with obvious hydrocephalus. This is so because most of the untreated cases do not survive beyond the early years of life and because those who are detected early and are treated successfully can expect normal head growth and appearance.

How is the diagnosis of hydrocephalus made?

In rare instances when the diagnosis of hydrocephalus is made *in utero* (inside the mother's womb), it is done by

X-ray pictures. These show the size of the head to be unusually large. After birth the size of the head can be measured and compared with the expected normal head size and rate of growth. Also it is useful to compare the size of the head with the size of the chest, since as a rule the circumference of the head is nearly the same as the circumference of the chest during the first year of life. If soon after birth the size of the head increases more rapidly than the size of the chest, the possibility of hydrocephalus must be considered.

At the same time, other abnormal features can be observed. For instance, bulging of the fontanels (or soft spots) suggests increased pressure inside the head. Your doctor will determine whether the soft spots are enlarged and whether the bones are farther apart than they should be. X-rays of the head will reveal separation of the skull bones from each other, and perhaps unusual thinning of the bones because of pressure. Sometimes the eyelids are pulled up by the stretched skin of the forehead. In such a case more of the whites of the eyes than usual can be seen. Also there may be a tendency for the eyes to turn down.

Finally, your doctor may advise certain tests which usually are done by a neurosurgeon. These tests often involve the removal of some of the fluid from the ventricles and the replacing of the fluid with air. X-ray pictures then will show abnormalities of size and shape of the ventricles and thus give the final diagnosis. This type of X-ray picture is called a ventriculogram—in other words, a picture of the ventricles of the brain by use of X-rays. The presence and severity of the hydrocephalus is thus determined. This procedure, which has relatively little danger in expert hands, must be done in all cases of progressive hydrocephalus.

What can be done for my child with hydrocephalus?

If the hydrocephalus is mild and is not showing any progression, your doctor may want to observe the infant for further developments. In a few instances the obstruction is only temporary, and the infant's head will resume normal growth without any special treatment. If the head definitely is enlarging more rapidly than the chest and there are other signs of hydrocephalus developing, the test described above should be made. As soon as a diagnosis is made and it is apparent that there is a severe or progressive hydrocephalus, a decision will be made by the neurosurgeon as to what should be done.

Many operations for hydrocephalus have been tried in the past fifty or more years. These have included the coagulation of or the surgical removal of a portion of the choroid plexuses that produce the cerebrospinal fluid. Although this procedure has some success, it requires a larger opening, and there may be some damage to the brain.

The newer shunting procedures are somewhat more successful than other surgical measures. In these operations a tube is inserted so that it will carry the spinal fluid away from the head. One end of the tube is placed in a ventricle above the obstruction. The other end is brought out beneath the scalp and then beneath the skin of the chest and into the body, where the cerebrospinal fluid can be taken care of with other body fluids. Various procedures have utilized various drainage areas for this fluid. Tiny valves are used sometimes within the shunting tubes to regulate the flow. It may be of some interest to you to know that one successfully used valve, the Holter valve, was invented by a machinist and engineer whose own child had hydrocephalus. He developed the valve in time for it to be of value to his own child!

Though there are a few complications which limit their use, these shunting operations are relatively simple, the risks involved are minor, and they have been amazingly successful in many children.

What are the chances for my child to be normal?

To know what kind of child the hydrocephalic child will be, we must determine the severity of the hydrocephalus and how much damage has been done to the brain before birth or by the time the disorder is recognized. If the trouble is treated early before the ventricles in the brain have become too enlarged the child may be perfectly normal. As the brain overlying the ventricles becomes thinner, the chance of some degree of mental retardation increases. After surgical treatment, the size of the head usually remains as it is until the body catches up with it, thereafter it grows at a normal rate. Many times, however, the head remains a little larger than normal.

The total picture of what the future will hold for your child will also depend on whether he has other abnormalities and the severity of such abnormalities.

The child probably will be normal mentally if the disease is successfully treated before there is excessive damage to the brain. Even in some instances in which the brain has been less than half an inch thick, the mentality has not been seriously affected. However, a child with a thin brain and large ventricles usually develops slowly and is mentally retarded. In some cases when damage takes place before birth, or develops rapidly after birth, the resulting damage to the brain is so severe that no operation will help. These babies remain like infants all their lives and usually die young. Those with fairly normal brains in which the ventricles have not become too large usually develop into normal, healthy infants and children both mentally and physically.

It is a matter of urgency, therefore, that the infant be successfully treated before the head becomes too enlarged, the ventricles too expanded, and the brain too thin.

Are scientists working on the problem of hydrocephalus?

Much work is being done in hospitals and research centers throughout the world on this perplexing problem. Advances in the past decade make it possible to salvage the majority of these infants. Still more improvement is essential, however, because no operation to date is anywhere near a hundred per cent effective in all cases—even those on whom treatment is started early. New types of valves, refinements in the valves we have, and improvements in the materials used are being studied every day. As new plastic and rubber materials become available, they are studied to be sure that the body will accept them and that they will cause no damage. One problem under close study is that of having to replace the shunts from time to time as the infant grows, for unfortunately the rubber or plastic tubing in present use does not grow with the infant.

Basic scientific research is going on continually so that more may be learned about what causes these abnormalities to develop in the unborn child, how the fluid is formed in the brain, how it is absorbed, what can be done to improve absorption or, if necessary, to decrease formation. It may take several years for a new type of treatment to be developed so that it can be put into general use. New materials, techniques, and procedures are first thoroughly tested on laboratory animals before being considered safe and useful for children.

What is the outlook for the treatment of hydrocephalus?

The outlook at the present is bright for even better solutions to the problem of hydrocephalus. Just where new research will lead us in this respect cannot be guessed, but there is reason to believe that every year a higher percentage of babies with hydrocephalus will have the opportunity to develop as normal children and eventually to become normal adults.